These Old Familiar Rooms

Mike Hornyak

The Henlo Press
Independent Publishing

Printed in the United States of America

First Printing, 2025

ISBN-978-1-962019-14-9

www.thehenlopress.com

The Henlo Press
P.O. Box 1694
Ashland, KY 41105

For Grandma Beautiful
You're in more of these stories than I realized when I wrote them.

And for Grandma & Grandpa Hornyak
You're in more of my memories than I realized when we made them.

Down the dark hall
    of my deep sleep
        where the past drops in like unwanted guests
Rattling their chains of thought
    shuffling their feet
        peering into things I thought I'd laid to rest
And for all I've left undone
    there's another dream to come

~Emily Saliers

Table of Contents

- *Introduction*

Part I:
Dreams We Visit

Part II:
Games We Play

Part III:
Homes We Build

Introduction

My mother has dreams about rooms. They started in her thirties, around the time I was born. She would dream about places from her past, curious passages and mysterious underground spaces. Hallways would extend endlessly before her eyes, lined with dozens of doors leading to rooms filled with wonders or guarding secrets.

She has always been fascinated by the idea of unknown compartments and what could be in them. There's a certain wonder that comes with entering a space that isn't your own. What will you find? What lies hidden, and why? If this room were yours, what would you do with it? A room's contents say so much about its inhabitant. Years from now, when we're gone, what would another explorer discover?

She thinks about the creation of rooms. They have to start somewhere: floors and framing, beams and battens. Suddenly, they're a house—filled with our hopes and desires, fears and fantasies. Many of her dreams involve a space forming around her, or scenery shifting suddenly from place to place.

She once described a dream in which her mother's best friend visited in a moving van. They unloaded a large desk and when they finally wrestled it inside, it turned into a piano. It seemed perfectly natural, but they had a hard time finding a place for it because the features and dimensions of the room itself kept changing.

I also have dreams about rooms. I've had them all my life. In my early twenties, my mother and I discovered this may be a family trait. I don't recall how it came up, but I remember the enchanting, uncanny feeling when we realized how many details our dreams had in common. Hidden rooms are a strong recurring theme, as well as taking strange and convoluted paths to find them. We also revisit the places we find.

More often than not, my dreams begin in one place, then I turn around and I'm somewhere else altogether. Sometimes I'll open a door and walk through to somewhere completely illogical. The earliest dream I can remember happened when I was five or six. Bad guys were chasing me through the house, so I crawled through the dryer and out into the backyard to escape. Ludicrous, indeed, but dreams are funny that way.

This collection explores that fascination with the mystery and endless potential of rooms. The stories, essays, and poems within represent those spaces and many more. Every dream, every feeling and every memory is a room. Every moment we observe and hide away fills a compartment. They create the architecture of our past and mark the map to the future. They can comfort us, bring us joy, haunt us, or trap us—the same as any four walls.

We visit these places from time to time, sometimes by our own will, sometimes by a whim of the heart or a trick of the mind. Our dreams take us when they need to, spiriting us away through the memories that build our lives.

Some memories welcome you with open doors, waiting near at hand. Some doors open like creaking garden gates, reluctant but cooperative. Some will hardly budge, but they can be coaxed if conditions are ideal. Some doors are simply locked forever—or are they?

Part I:

Dreams We Visit

The House on the Hill
(Part I)

"Don't cry. There's always a way.
Here in November, in this house of leaves, we pray.
Please, I know it's hard to believe —
to see a perfect forest through so many splintered trees.
You and me, and these shadows keep on changing."
~ from "Haunted" by Annie Danielewski

She strolled through a field of tall wheat, tufted stalks brushing against her hips. The crop and soil stirred a nutty, earthy aroma that filled her senses. A low whistle of soft breeze and a distant chorus of cicadas clung to the evening air. The mix was comforting like home, yet mournful like a memory she couldn't touch.

Wading and wandering without much sense of direction, she ran her hands over the tops of the stalks, feeling the smooth kernels pass between her fingers. The field rolled out in front of her, a seemingly endless landscape. Trees on the horizon suggested bordering woods, but they never appeared to get any closer.

Open spaces made her nervous, a fact she remembered slowly. It seemed to creep in from the sidelines. She couldn't quite put her finger on why she was in that field in the first place or how she got there, but she wasn't frightened. She was acutely intrigued.

She looked behind her, measuring how far she had come. A fence with a small opening hung far behind her, but much too close for how long it felt that she had been ambling along. The prickling questions of how and why begged again. Still, there was nothing for it but to continue her journey.

After a few moments, mesmerized by the swaying of that gray-golden sea, she noticed something in her periphery. In the very near distance, a large white farmhouse sat atop a wide hill that rose modestly from the boundless field. It was a pretty house and despite its aged and weathered paint, it looked brilliant against the gray sky. *Home, at last?*

As she approached the hill, the wheat began to thin, tapering into a grassy lawn. Through the middle of the lawn ran a narrow dirt path, which led to a great veranda. Up the path she went, then on to the house. A wooden porch swing creaked quietly on its chains as she stood at the front door.

This place was familiar. It looked like something from a painting she had seen a million times, but she couldn't remember where. It felt like someplace she had been before, but she couldn't remember when. Nevertheless, it was clear that she was meant to visit this house and curiosity compelled her forward.

She stepped into a spacious living room. *What a charming house.* The rooms were much bigger and brighter than she assumed they would be from the outside. The walls were all a buttery cream and the furniture was lush and welcoming. She had a strong sense that she was home, yet she didn't fully recognize anything. This was certainly her house, though it didn't look like it.

On one side of the main room was a carpeted stairway leading to the second floor. On the other side, an archway opened into a substantial dining room connected to a kitchen that stretched to the back of the house.

She walked through the kitchen into a long, narrow room, lined with tall windows that looked out onto the yard and surrounding fields. In the middle of the windowed wall was the back door. She opened it and walked through, but rather than stepping outside, she found herself in the living room of an entirely different house.

This house was older, with mostly wooden floors and walls. There was some simple wallpaper and the occasional coat of paint, both peeling a bit here and there. It was furnished, but sparse. It was dusty and unkept, but not dirty. It was a bit run down, but not decrepit. *Perhaps it was abandoned?* It reminded her of an old dollhouse that hadn't been played with in decades. There was something sad about it, forlorn—and increasingly unsettling.

She knew it was no longer her home, but still felt as though she knew that place, like she belonged there. However, she did not feel the need to linger. It took a moment to realize, but the hum of the wind and the drone of cicadas were gone. Suddenly, the silence was palpable and the novelty of her adventure was wearing off. She still wasn't afraid, but common sense nudged her onward. *Where was she? Why was she there?*

Across the room, a door stood ajar. It was a good place to start, or at least a step toward a way out. Either way, it was an invitation she accepted. She crossed the room and ran her hand along the open edge, pulling it slowly toward her as she peeked in. The door creaked open, revealing a long corridor with doors to more than a dozen rooms.

Many of the doors were open, at least enough that she could tell what the rooms were as she walked by. Some were bedrooms, some were nurseries. Then there was a playroom and a room with a desk and typewriter. *How many people lived here?*

Some of the doors were closed. One or two let her inside and the rooms were just as mundane as the others, but a few of them were locked. Against her better judgment, she tried to force them but they refused to open. Her arms ached and her fingers went numb as she released the stubborn door handles, as if they had fought against her attempts.

Eventually, she came to a door that was half open, like somebody had swung it shut, but it bounced back. Nothing appeared to be special about it, but she felt a weight around her as she approached. She stopped for a moment, then stepped forward to look inside. The weight became worry. She couldn't help putting her hand on the door and pushing it a bit farther, revealing a large, sparsely furnished room.

A rocking horse rested beneath a tall, open window with thin, gauzy curtains that swayed listlessly. Carved spinning tops and jacks lay scattered on a wide braided rug. Further in, she glimpsed an armoire, a shaving table, and a four post canopy bed, all made of dull, dark wood. The bed had plain white linens and a lace dust ruffle. *Such a stark and joyless room.*

As she considered the room, the urge to explore its mysteries grew, as did the feeling of worry. It had turned into dread, buzzing in her chest and upsetting her stomach. She stepped forward but before she made it past the door frame, something unseen pushed her back. She leaned forward again, but this force would not let her enter. It had an iron grip on her, moving her from one side to the other, lifting her like a rag doll. She didn't know whether she should try to fight past it or pull back and escape.

She tried to yell, to call out and ask it to stop, but her voice got caught in the back of her throat with all of her breath. Something was protecting that room and whatever it was, it was much stronger than her. She couldn't fight it. She no longer had control of her body.

She woke up panicked and gasping, adrenaline surging as she thrashed herself free from an invisible weight. She shot upright and pushed herself back against the headboard, grasping her chest. Her lips and hands tingled as her senses caught up to her open, blurry eyes.

She got ahold of herself and looked around. Her blankets had all been thrown to the floor and her sheets were halfway off the bed, tangled and matted. *So dramatic...*

In her post-waking haze, she almost felt silly. It was just a dream, after all. She felt relief at having woken, but that sense of worry lingered for a long time. After all, she believed dreams can carry significance, and *that* had been quite the dream. Though she couldn't have known it then, this was not the last time she would visit that house.

Houses Into Hallways

"I'm haunted by the lies that I have loved and actions I have hated.
Haunted by the promises I've made and others I have broken.
Haunted by the hallways in this tiny room,
the echo there of me and you –
the voices that are carrying this tune…"
~ from "Haunted," by Annie Danielewski

Long day.
Finally home.
Get to see him.

I parked my car, unbuckled my seatbelt and took a breath.
Resting my head back against my seat, I looked through my
windshield at my house—only feet away, but it felt so far. It was
just a half an hour until he would be there, but every stubborn
minute of that drive dragged like a toddler digging in its heels.

With a click and creak, I opened my door, got out of the car
and stretched. I shut the door and glanced down to line my key up
with the metal lock. When I looked up, I was in the parking lot of
an outdoor mall. I was back at work. I had never seen that place
before, but I knew with certainty that it was where I worked.

What kind of fresh hell is this?

Storefronts and fancy facades stretched down a wide, divided
avenue. Small, tailored trees and posh statuary lined the sidewalks
—but there was something missing. It was mid-afternoon on a
Friday and there were no people in that beautiful mall.

Why am I here? I'm supposed to be seeing him right now.

As I walked, purpose slowly crept back in. Rationalization became intention: we were obviously supposed to be meeting at a restaurant. But which one? This place should be full of them.

No money.
How will we eat?
Get to see him.

I noticed quickly that there were no restaurants where the restaurants should be. They had all been replaced by one shop or another. Having never been to this particular mall, I also wondered how I knew anything about it at all. This was getting strange, and I felt like I was running out of time.

As it turned out, my never-could-have-been-favorite Italian restaurant had been replaced by an office for a dating service. *"FindLove"* was sprawled in golden cursive on the illuminated sign —the obnoxious kind, with hearts replacing the 'o' and the dot over the 'i.'

Maybe they'll know where he's gotten to.

I walked through the door and immediately stepped onto the sidewalk of a long street lined with small ranch style houses, leading into an expansive neighborhood. It was late afternoon so there was still daylight, but all of the streetlights were lit, making the street look even longer. I could smell the evening sneaking up.

I was outside, but I was also inside. I walked down the sidewalk looking at those houses, while at the same time, I had a strong sense that I was walking down a long hallway looking at doors, as if I were walking around a hotel. All of the sounds around me were dull as well, like they were muffled by walls and carpet.

He must be in one of these houses. God, this is just like him...

I made my way from house to house, opening each door and looking inside. Every house had an identical interior and somehow, with a cursory glance, I could tell he wasn't there. One after another, again and again, I searched.

This is getting ridiculous.

Day faded into night like a movie scene, blue sky swept away by gradients of rich purples and deep black. The clouds moved quickly from left to right, chased closely by stars, slightly staggered as if someone were pulling a rope to rotate scenery somewhere offstage. I could almost hear the pulleys squeak. All in one moment, I had been searching all day.

So many houses.
Running out of time.
Need to see him.

After quite a while, I came to a two-story house. This had to be the one. It just had to. I walked up the driveway, up the porch steps, and touched my fingers to the door handle.

Dear Lord, let this be the one.

I sighed, opened the door, and entered into a large, modestly decorated parlor. A fire crackled in a brick fireplace across the room. To the right, a staircase led to the second floor and landed at an opening that appeared to lead to a hallway.

I climbed the stairs and turned down the hall. It seemed to go on forever. A corridor this length could never have fit in a house this size. I looked behind me and the doorway had disappeared. The corridor stretched behind me as well. I started to feel uneasy, yet still had the sense that I was close to something.

The doors along the walls were plain wood and each opened into a bedroom. Every room had identical decor but a different color pallet. Every room was empty.

The uneasy feeling grew and I had all but given up hope when I came across a door that was unlike the others. This one was large, like the front door to a nice house. It was painted red, but like cinnamon, and hung with a boxwood wreath dotted with frosted pinecones.

Well, this seems odd…

I turned the substantial golden doorknob and poked my head into a bedroom, smaller than the others, and completely different. This bedroom was mine. And there he was—fully dressed, shoes on, napping on my bed.

Indeed, just like him…

He snored softly as I watched him for a moment, then I made my way over to the bed. He stirred slightly as I took off his shoes. I placed them by the bed, accompanied by my own, then laid down next to him, closed my eyes, and woke up.

Trial & Error

I try to riddle out these dreams.
I've been having them again, night after night.
Why does your face appear to me
after all this time?

I try to pick apart these lies
that I've believed and I have told, again and again.
What is it now that's binding me
to what I did then?

And I feel this old, familiar pull —
and it's cold. Oh, it's so cold.
The houses turn to hallways on the path that I chose.
Then I trip, and I falter on my road.

I've tried to get gone my past.
All the things that I have done and the faces I have shown.
Why do you have to push me there
when I can do that on my own?

I try to take apart these fears —
the ghosts around my head that are keeping me cold.
Why do you step away from me
when I need you to hold?

And I feel that old, familiar pull —
and it's cold. You know it's so cold.
The houses turn to hallways on the path that I chose.
Then I trip, and I falter on my road.

I try to take apart these fears.
Why won't you walk away from me?
Why do you pull me close to you
and kiss me like you do?

For Jake

The Horse Girl & the Stairway to Nowhere
(Part I)

A symphony of crickets and mourning doves wove a somber enchantment through the woods. The clumsy ask-and-answer of chirping frogs crooned a delicate lullaby. There was no wind, no distant hum of civilization, only the sounds of the forest and her own footsteps.

She walked along a narrow path. A small creek ran alongside to her right, its mossy, rocky banks separating the trail from a deep expanse of forest. The burbling, flirtatious murmur of the water begged her senses—a cool, soothing promise.

The sun was low in the morning sky, casting long, gentle shadows through the woodland canopy. It slowly softened the crisp edge of the new-day air. Evaporating dew carried the scent of drowsy flora and rich earth.

Surrounded as she was by nature's encompassing solitude, it alarmed her to realize she wasn't alone. On the other side of the stream and several yards into the trees, a young woman on horseback strode into her periphery. The woman was well dressed, with fair skin and long dark hair, and though she tried, she couldn't see the young woman's face.

Her view was mottled by leaves and shade. It was hazy and surreal, like she was watching something that wasn't quite there, a memory or a dream, but not her own. She watched the horse and its traveler saunter through the trees, and while they took no notice of her, she couldn't take her eyes off of them. Suddenly self-conscious, she slowed her pace and let them continue slightly ahead.

The longer they walked along, the less it seemed like reality, though she couldn't help feeling they were there for a reason. A sense of familiarity blossomed within her, but with it grew a little sadness. She knew that girl, but she didn't know why. She even recognized the dress cascading down the horse's flank. She would love to have worn that dress—she could almost feel it against her skin.

It dawned on her like she had known it all along, but it occurred slowly, as if someone had been whispering a long secret. She was the girl on that horse. She was watching her younger self riding a horse she never had, on a walk she never took, in beautiful clothes she never wore. That realization carried a rueful poignance, as if she were being shown a path not taken or possibilities that never came to be. Potential unreached. How might her life have been? Who could she have been and what would she have done? Silly questions, really, though one can never help to wonder.

Her pace slowed again, or maybe the horse's gait increased—she couldn't tell which. She tried to walk faster, but the path had other ideas. The ground itself seemed to resist her stride as she fell further and further behind. She was losing them and though she understood the absurdity of her panic, it felt like something important was slipping away.

With a heavy sigh she looked away and shook her head, an action born of sadness and frustration, which quickly became a merciful breath of clarity. Breaking her concentration on the horse and its rider, the trance they had cast weakened.She wasn't unhappy with the life she had lived. While the thought of what could have been would linger like burnt incense, it would never be more than that.

When she returned her gaze across the stream, the horse had traveled even farther ahead. She smiled wistfully as she watched them walk slowly into the distance. It was back to her own path. The horse and young woman went on along their journey. Their trail curved off and they continued through the trees and out of sight.

Dried Roses & Powder

It always took forever to fall asleep at grandma's house. It wasn't very often that I got to spend the night with her, so it stands out amid the memories of singing and cooking, playing board games and watching PBS mysteries.

Her old sofa was fine for sitting, but not for sleeping and even as a child, I've never been fully comfortable in places that weren't my own. I would drift off eventually, but most times, after hours of half-sleep, her sweet little sheltie would come check on me. The jingle of her collar would be just enough to bring me around.

This particular night was no exception. On the sofa, in the dark stillness of her living room, the dead silence gave way to the ticking of every clock in her house, and, it seemed, the clocks of all her neighbors. That delicate but relentless tick-tick-tocking was difficult to ignore.

After a fair amount of time, the constant ticks blended together—each consecutive sound stirring a hypnotic mix—and lulled me to sleep.

When I woke, the light was dim and soft, diffused through white sheer curtains, and warmed by the drapes. I rubbed my eyes, letting them adjust to the new daylight and rose from the sofa to check the time.

8:25

Everything was still and quiet, apart from the faint and faraway singing of birds in the trees and fields that surrounded the property. In fact, it was dead silent in the house—no footsteps, no water running, no furnace blowing and no clocks ticking. I remember thinking it was odd, even as a little boy, that all of the clocks seemed to have stopped.

I walked into the dining room, the kitchen, the laundry room, the guest room, even the foyer—it was all the same: complete silence and no one to be found. Out the front door I could see there were no cars in the driveway. I was only five or six and I was

16

all alone, but the uneasy feeling in my stomach gave way quickly when I realized something much more important.

This can only mean one thing, I thought. *I was sure this day would never come.*

I get to play in grandma's closet.

Back through the living room, I went to her bedroom doorway and walked in apprehensively. After glancing around and checking her bathroom, just in case, I opened the closet door and stepped inside. The chain pull to the light fixture was just above my reach so I hopped to pull it, then shut the door behind me.

I took a moment to survey my surroundings. The closet was a rectangle, deeper than wide—modest, but strangely bigger on the inside than her bedroom seemed to have room for. Everything was perfectly organized, except a few stacks of bins and hat boxes. On the floor, her shoes lined the walls, layered on several racks, each one resting on a wire hill. Above, blouses and skirts hung on each opposite wall, while coats and dresses occupied the far wall.

I filed through everything, swishing hangers back and forth, running my hands over the fabrics. I imagined my grandma doing that while she picked her outfits.

When I got to the back of the closet, I could feel a subtle, cool air current around my feet, as if the air conditioning had turned on. There weren't any vents on the floor, yet the hems of the coats and dresses stirred slightly. I knelt down to see where it was coming from, but found nothing.

Still, the dresses swayed and I began to hear a low whistling sound that seemed to come from directly in front of me. I put my hands between two garments and pushed them apart, revealing the wall behind them. There, I discovered the source.

Nearly two feet off the ground, there was a hole in the wall. It wasn't a hole like one that would be made by a hammer, or that somebody punched, breaking the plaster and splintering the wood. It was more like an opening, round and deliberate, almost like a hollow in a tree. It was small enough to hide behind her clothes, but large enough that I could look inside.

Curiosity had its way and I cautiously placed my hands on the lower rim of the opening and looked inside, letting myself in about nose deep. There were no lights inside, but I could see everything perfectly. The opening led to a tunnel. It looked like the inside of a wall, lined with plaster and bits of wood with pink insulation stuffed everywhere, but it extended several feet out and curved off, leading to who knows where.

As if it had been the whole time, the opening was now shoulder wide and I was able to crawl in. I had no idea where it would take me, but I was compelled onward. After crawling through for a moment, the tunnel curved upward, but not so steeply that I couldn't struggle my way through.

A few feet more and I came to the other end of the tunnel, crawling out hands first into a small room, not much larger than the closet I had left only minutes before. I appeared to be in some kind of dressing room. It was beautiful, like nothing I had ever seen. There were things everywhere, but it wasn't messy and everything was slightly dusty. No one had been here in a while. The air smelled like dried roses and old powder…and a little perfume.

The first thing I noticed was a chair that had faded pink crushed velvet cushions in front of a small vanity. Its mirror was a tall floating oval, framed in lights. All around, there were hundreds of delicate baubles and delicious trinkets.

On a woven, tasseled mat in the middle of the table, there was an ornate silver hand mirror and a mother of pearl hairbrush. Two crystal perfume bottles with leather bulbs stood among an array of ivory barrettes and hair combs. A gilded floral powder box sat next to a rouge compact and its bronze brush.

To one side of the table were trays full of antique cameos, lustrous brooches and various rings and pins. On the other, a tin chest filled with marbles and odd buttons sat behind an open box of partially used grease paint makeup sticks. Against the mirror, strands of pearls, beaded strings, and golden chains dangled from a pewter necklace tree like a bejeweled willow.

Shawls, cloth, and velvet swaths hung about like wallpaper. In the corner next to the vanity, a mannequin bust was draped with silk scarves and feather boas. This could have been the dressing room of a ballerina or a vaudevillian actress—but however enchanting it was, there was something faraway and wistful about it.

I've been to that room more than once. On at least one more occasion, I found myself back in grandma's bedroom, in search of a path to that place. I can't help but wonder if she somehow let me in on a secret, a place inside her that she kept hidden from the world. Did she go there when she needed to retreat from her daily responsibilities, gazing into that lighted mirror and daydreaming about a glamorous life?

Perhaps, she had a secret life. Perhaps, she had been a dancer —a painted, perfumed showgirl, twirling plumes and sparkling in the eyes of her adoring fans. Maybe her mother was secretly a famous ballerina and she kept that piece of her safe, visiting for quiet moments or silly makeup adventures like when she was a little girl.

Maybe they were just dreams. Though, in my experience, there isn't any such thing.

We all have hidden rooms.

Wild Strawberries

Smoke lingers from so many candles.
Curls and queues hang and shift so slightly.
A languid dance, almost dead in the stillness of the air,
but the dim glow of wick ends' dying light makes it look alive.
A fleeting little light, carried away by the wind with the smoke…
                                    and another birthday.

I remember picking wild strawberries.
A vague, sun-golden memory of the sand dunes at Oak Openings.
Amid the bramble and Earthstars,
    all the secret places my mother knew.
Then again, we might have picked them
    behind the shed in our backyard.
Memories are funny that way.
They turned up on my birthday cake,
placed between perfect rosettes of white icing around the border.
                                    It had a mermaid on it.

I remember picking wild people.
Quiet, careful creatures—shy and magical, hiding their light.
Brazen, bristling beasts—fierce and protective, hiding their hearts.
The most beautiful blossoms, rare and endangered.
Flowers are funny that way.
They turn up in the strangest places.
Amid the bramble, you can find them if you look hard enough—
                                    when you care enough.

I remember loving wild winds.
Blustering hurricanes: passionate tempests
   who strike above your guard.
Raging typhoons: feral storms
   who level your world and fuck your skies.
Soft breezes: gentle zephyrs who dance a comforting seduction.
Wind is funny that way—
all currents and eddies, building to magnificent elemental forces
Or fading into nothing—an unavoidable passing. Vanishing…
                                                            Leaving.

I remember drinking alone.
Another year I didn't earn. There's nothing like another milestone.
Another celebration I didn't deserve.
   There's nothing like another reminder.
My beautiful flowers, wherever they were,
   lost in the bramble again.
Friends are funny that way.
I remember a life waiting at empty tables.
A life carried away with the wind.
            Like smoke from so many candles…
                              and another birthday.

Barn Dance

She walked quickly down the street, a sense of immediacy driving her toward a destination that was not yet clear. The scenery changed around her, and she started to lose track of where she was. Home had been near, but she was no longer certain and nighttime was closing in. She walked faster and faster until she found herself running. There was nobody around to threaten her, though it felt like she was being chased.

An old, dilapidated barn sat a short way off the road in a grassy field. She ran inside and paused to catch her breath. It was dark, but a bit of moonlight made its way through the aging boards. After a moment, she decided to explore, looking for places to hide and additional ways out.

Toward the back of the barn, a long ladder led up through an open square hatch—as good a lead as any. When she tested the wood, it creaked and complained. Some of the rungs turned in their sockets. It wasn't particularly safe, but urgency overrode any sense of self-preservation.

She climbed and climbed that rickety ladder, gaining very little distance from the ground. All the while, it wobbled as she struggled to keep her hold. Eventually, she passed through the open hatch and into a hay loft. As she continued upward, the structure of the ladder became less and less sound. By the time she reached the next opening, it had all but fallen apart.

Barely managing to get her head and arms through the opening, the ladder gave way completely. She leveraged one final push against the wood, securing her torso while she pulled and kicked the rest of her body up and onto the floor. She laid there for a moment, took a deep breath, and sighed heavily.

She was in a large, open room with smooth hardwood floors. The walls were lined with built-in shelves filled with hundreds of books and records. Candles were lit all over the room, providing the only light besides a tall floor lamp in the far corner. In front of the lamp was an overstuffed leather chair that rested on a shaggy rug. A small round table with a record player sat at its arm.

She loved that room. It was comfortable and homely. Fascinated by the collections on the walls, she searched and inspected. Which records did their owner love? What books lived on those shelves?

Other than the decadent satisfaction of exploration, there was little to be discovered. All of the titles were in a language she didn't recognize and the album covers had images she couldn't quite discern, like dusty paintings that wouldn't come into focus.

Along the wall at the end of her investigation, an open doorway leading to a flight of stairs suggested a path to another level. With a final glance around the room, she climbed again.

It was as if she had been transported back to the 1950s. This room was well lit and the decor was sleek and streamlined, minimal but still quite rich. It had turquoise carpeting and white tiled walls adorned with square clocks, and a big, golden sunburst mirror. In the middle of the room was a curvy, mustard-colored sofa and matching lounge chair on either side of an angular wooden coffee table with slender, tapered legs.

It was a lot to take in, but she felt at home. She was reminded of her grandmother's house: post-war modern but warm and friendly. She wanted to lay down and process everything, but her attention was diverted. An iron spiral staircase had appeared in an open area behind the sofa. It clearly led to yet another level and she could only imagine what awaited her this time.

She emerged from the landing of the staircase and into a room that was larger and much deeper than the others. This space was an image of elegance. The floors were polished marble, swirled in black and white. The high walls were lined with columns and between them were tall, arched windows that let in bright daylight that made the marble glow. The last windows on each wall were open.

The room was completely silent. She could hear her heartbeat, and as she began to walk, every footstep echoed. It felt like she was in a museum, yet somehow she belonged there.

The only furnishing was a huge, almost Brobdingnagian mahogany desk that stood alone in the center of the room. On the far wall was an opulent fireplace. She crossed the room and traced her fingers over the lines of its intricate carvings, admiring every detail.

A mild breeze wandered in from the open window to her right, reminding her that she had been looking for a way out. As she approached, she noticed a glint from below. A few metal jacks and a red rubber ball lay on the floor in front of the window. *How strange.*

When she poked her head out the window, it was nighttime again. In an instant, the sunlight had gone completely. Confused and slightly alarmed, she decided it was time to go. She looked around to see if there was a convenient way to leave. To her relief, the window overlooked a small, flat area of roof with a hint of wooden trellis peeking up over the edge.

She climbed out and onto the roof. The moon was notably close, like it had been painted directly onto the sky, creating a ghostly blue ambiance. When she surveyed her surroundings, it was clear that instead of the old barn, she was on the roof of a farmhouse looking out over a wide field of short crops.

In the near distance, she could see the road where everything started. Utterly bewildered and eager to move along, she went to the edge of the roof, carefully climbed onto the trellis, and scaled down the side of the house. Once she reached the ground, she walked quickly across the yard and off through the field toward home.

Enter, Stage Right

I used to have dreams about traveling with my father. We never seemed to be going anywhere specific or doing anything noteworthy. We simply arrived at places we hadn't been and explored. It reminded me of going on summer trips with our family in my grandpa's old van.

It was typically mundane. Whenever we walked into a gas station or rest stop, I would suddenly be somewhere else. Sometimes, a door appeared where I didn't expect a door to be. Naturally, I would investigate and once again be transported away.

We once stopped at a restaurant. I got up to find the restroom, though when I opened the door, it was not a restroom that waited for me. It was always the same. No matter where I started out, I always ended up in the auditorium of my elementary school.

The dream I remember most vividly took place at a motel. My grandparents and my aunts had gone to one room while my father, my uncle, and I went to another. Our room was a small chamber with a stone floor and cedar walls. It looked more like a tiny sauna than a motel room.

There was nothing there except for two cedar benches built out from the walls to our left and right, and a narrow door in the far wall between them. I remember thinking there had to be more space somewhere, so I dropped my bags on one of the benches and opened the door, hoping to find an adjoining room or at least a large closet. I walked through and found myself, once again, in the auditorium.

It was a small gymnasium in an old brick schoolhouse, consisting of a hardwood basketball floor, flanked on one side by a stage set into the wall about four feet off the ground. On the other side was a steep wall of uncomfortable wooden theater seats. It had been the setting of many a quaint (though somewhat embarrassing) grade school concert.

Occasionally, I entered the auditorium through the front doors, looking down at the stage and gym floor from the top of the seating area. I would walk slowly down the steps and run my hands along the tops of the chipped wooden chairs, remembering the times I spent there for school events or rehearsing for performances.

Most times, I entered through a doorway to the steps that led up from the dressing room into the right wing, looking out onto the stage. I would take the short stairway, my hand on the old pipe railing, and walk out. It was worn and slightly warped in places, just as I remembered. Standing on the stage and looking out at the auditorium brought waves of nostalgia. Still, there's something a little sad about an empty theater, and it was strange being there alone.

I think about those dreams from time to time, though I haven't had them in years. The seemingly random juxtaposition of the auditorium and my family vacations still puzzles me. I've always been curious how the two connected, or if they are connected at all.

After all, they say everything that happens in dreams means something, however insignificant. But I wonder.

Dreams

I had a dream once
I dreamt of a quiet place
      with nothing but myself and the distant singing birds
      with nothing but quiet thoughts of you

I had a dream once
I dreamt of a quiet place
      where the streams ran clear after years of poison
      where life returned to the jaded ground

I had a dream once
I dreamt you were with me
      here, in quiet places with breeze blown willows
      here, in the stillness, the amaranthine peace

I had a dream once
A dream of a quiet place
      with breezy willows and singing birds, crystal streams
      with you, smiling in soft sunlight

I had a dream once
A dream with you in a quiet place
      One day, I'll return

The Ghost in the Grain
(The House on the Hill: Part II)

She walked barefoot along the edge of a gravel road. She was on her way, yet the path led nowhere in particular. Hours seemed to pass as she navigated the quiet pastoral trails she knew so well—such abiding friends.

Tiger lilies spattered vivid orange upon the dense shade of the trees that lined the road, and it was a long road—the kind that gartered fields and bordered farmland. The rich, earthy smell of leaves and distant verdure saturated the air and followed the breeze, the only mercy in that evening's heat, which was quite sure of itself.

The sun was setting, but it went down fighting. It was the kind of late summer day in southern Michigan that gathered steam from all the lakes and pushed it directly against her. The air was thick and heavy, but she didn't mind. The ground was cool under her feet, and her sundress caught the breeze and fluttered about, soothing her skin.

Through a break in the trees, a moldering split rail fence waited near. It old and familiar, with a narrow gap that opened into a vast, rolling field of wheat. Not far in the distance, a large white farmhouse stood on a grassy hill that rose up awkwardly from the middle of that crested pasture. The deep hues of sunset and hanging haze of humidity made it look like a mirage, an oasis in a golden desert.

Through the fence and into the sea of gilded crop she went. The tufted stalks brushed against her hips and she ran her fingers over their smooth kernels as she waded along, lost in her thoughts and intoxicated by the gentle drone of cicadas. It didn't take long to reach the house on the hill, or maybe it did.

The wheat thinned and tapered away into a grassy lawn as she approached the house. She went up a narrow dirt path to the front door and nodded to the porch swing that greeted her.

She walked into a charming, spacious living room with cozy furniture. Through an archway to her left, there was a beautiful dining room. As if she were following a map, she moved through the dining room into a long kitchen that led back to a lengthy, narrow room lined with windows that looked out on the back yard.

She opened a door in the middle of the windowed wall and went through, finding herself in the living room of another house. This house was older, darker, and sparsely furnished. It was slightly run down and unkept but not dirty. It had clearly been abandoned. There was something sad about it, and a bit unsettling. *I know this place.* She had been there before, though she couldn't put her finger on why. Nevertheless, she was compelled forward.

She walked across the room to a door that stood ajar. She ran her hand along the open edge, pushing it slowly away from her as she peeked in. The door creaked open, revealing a long hallway with doors to more than a dozen rooms. *Here we go again.* The sense of familiarity crept deeper, and she began to understand.

The hallway had changed. It was longer than she remembered, and the rooms and doors were different. Some doors were open, but most were closed—many more than last time, as if the house was trying to keep more and more secrets. Although curious, she couldn't shake a sense of foreboding that loomed ever closer as she continued down the corridor. As she walked past, the air felt thick around every closed door, like a silent warning.

Through the dread, she reasoned that whatever was trying to keep her away from those rooms may have been there to protect what was inside. This thought was accompanied by what she could only describe as a wave of affection, a deep maternal understanding of the instinct to shield something precious. That comfort, however, was undermined by a persisting sense of trepidation. It also occurred to her that the force may be there for her own protection, a chilling thought in that inscrutable house.

She approached the end of the hallway. Only a few steps more, each one slower than the next, and she was there—that certain door, waiting half-open. Once again, she looked into a large, modest bedroom. A rocking horse sat against a wall near an open window with thin, gauzy curtains that swayed drowsily. A few toys lay scattered on a wide braided rug. To the side, she glimpsed a couple of posts from a canopy bed made of dull, dark wood with plain white linens and a lace dust ruffle. *Such a stark and joyless room.*

As though she were in a trance, her arm raised and pushed the door inward. Her body moved toward the open door without hesitation as a growing fear buzzed in her chest and made her stomach churn. She knew what was coming.

Before she made it inside, an invisible force pushed her away. She fought back, throwing her shoulder forward and bracing her other arm on the doorframe, but it had surrounded her. It pinned her arms to her side and lifted her off the ground. The pressure was so great, she found it hard to breathe.

The harder she fought, the more the atmosphere excited. The rocking horse rocked, and the curtains billowed. She struggled against it, kicking and shifting her weight, teeth clenched and adrenaline raging. Something was protecting that room, and whatever it was, it was stronger than her—but this would not be like the other times.

Terror surged from her core, but determination armed her. From her sides, she forced her arms out and kicked against the floor in a defiant burst, tearing herself free from the invisible oppressor and lurching forward through the door frame. Full of momentum, she tumbled to her hands and knees. Her pounding heart boomed in her ears, and her chest heaved as her lungs once again filled with air.

It took a moment to find her bearings, but eventually she rose to her feet. She was finally in the room but had no idea what that meant. The threatening force had gone, yet a feeling of worry lingered. She didn't belong there; she felt it distinctly. She didn't even want to be there, so she turned to head back to the door.

A young Black boy stood on the rug farther into the room. He was around 10 years old, as far as she could tell. His figure was vague, and her eyes couldn't quite focus. When she tried to look directly at him, it was like looking into a bright light. She couldn't discern many details, though she squinted and angled her head as if the sun were in her eyes.

She hadn't had much time to consider him when he turned suddenly and ran away through the open window. Incredulous and startled, she hurried to the window and looked out onto the empty lawn sloping downward to the wheat field. The little boy was nowhere to be seen. *What just happened here?*

Was he the imposing force that was protecting the room? Could it have been the boy who was being protected? Perhaps it was both. These questions would haunt her for a long time.

There are some things that we're not meant to see, some rooms we're not supposed to visit. Some secrets should remain secret.

She never returned to that house.

They're Aliens, You Know...

EXT. COUNTRY ROAD - SUNSET

Two parents and their son drive down a dirt road. Dust kicks up from their wheels and hangs in the air, adding to a dramatic, lonesome vista. Deep in farm country, the landscapes offer what you would expect of them, but magnified by the dying light and rainbow sherbet sky.

Out the passenger side windows, the family notices a seemingly endless field. It's relatively flat, having been recently harvested—leftover stems of its crop have created a jagged, unseemly carpet.

Resting sporadically throughout the field are dozens of giant rolls of hay.

> MOM
> They're aliens, you know...

> ME
> I should have guessed.

> MOM
> It's obvious, once you know.

> DAD
> It's hard to come to any other conclusion with the available evidence.

MOM

It's clear as day.

ME

Well, it's a great disguise.

MOM

Oh, that's not a disguise! It's just the way they look.

ME

I love that. They're beautiful. But they just look like rolled hay.

DAD

Space hay.

ME

But why are they here? What do they want? If they're alive, what do they even do? What do they eat?

MOM

If we knew what they did when we weren't looking, they wouldn't be doing a good job blending in. Would they?

ME

I guess not.

MOM

And they eat mostly corn.

DAD

Space corn.

MOM

They do a lot of traveling and they noticed the way we harvest our crops. Our empty fields remind them of home. They come here to rest.

ME

I love that. They look lonely, though. I hope they're not lonely.

DAD

Everyone's alone when they sleep.

MOM

They're not lonely. They're just here until they're ready to leave.

ME

If they're just visiting aliens, why do I always see them stacked on the back of trucks on the highway?

DAD

That's how they get back to their spaceships.

ME *(thinking)*
Is "spaceships" politically correct?

MOM

They have an arrangement with the U.S. Department of Agriculture.

ME

Ah! Well, good for them!

MOM

They do seem content.

DAD

It's hard to come to any other conclusion with the available evidence.

Cureless Autumn

Cool breezes float through my window
  They break upon my face,
    waiting eagerly to ease the heat within

Everywhere, the autumn trees are in a blaze
  Yellow, orange, brilliant red
    against the blue-gray yonder

Below me, the leaf-covered ground
  waits impatiently for
    careless, cureless feet

The branches of the trees outside
  look cold and brittle and jaded—
    like my hands, who have no companion…
        no source of warmth but my empty pockets

Dull sunlight from behind the clouds
    illuminates what is left
      of the mid-evening day
          Break of dusk is near

This season suspends the world
    A breath before the loneliness of winter
      Even the trees get to stop and sleep
          But we endure and know
            this won't be all there is

Originally written in Autumn '04
Revised in Summer 2023

The Horse Girl & the Stairway to Nowhere
(Part II)

It felt like she had been walking for hours. The narrow woodland path she took seemed to go on and on. Even the playful, burbling stream to her right sounded tired. Perhaps it was the weight of introspection that had gotten to her. Perhaps it was the strain of puzzling out the purpose of her journey. Either way, she continued. That was, however, until something caught her eye.

She approached a small set of stone steps built into a shallow slope three or four yards off to the left of her path. They were weathered and uneven, cracked and crumbling in a few places. She surmised they were well over a hundred years old. Several trees and various flora formed a shady archway over them, their dense branches creating a leafy awning.

The steps appeared to lead up, but to nowhere in particular. She reasoned that they may have led to a small bridge crossing a gully or creek that had since dried or been filled in. Or maybe at one point, the trail simply diverged and went up the slope to continue. Now, roots disrupted the top few steps and plants had grown a wall that sealed off whatever opening was once there.

She felt a pull toward the steps. Such a beautiful and curious little woodland oddity was hard to ignore. She wanted to climb them. The urge was almost irresistible. They had an air of mystery and magic. They had a history. They knew things. More than that, they led somewhere. She could feel it.

She could only think that the young woman on the horse had led her to this place. There had to be a reason. Giving into the mystery, she turned from her path and went to the tiny stairway.

Rather than the line of trees and tangled shrubs that could be seen from the path below, there was an opening at the top of the steps. It revealed a long, straight trail, lined on either side by tall trees and thick, vibrant undergrowth. The branches of the trees curved upward and inward, forming a vaulted canopy—an endless, narrow cathedral.

Through the opening and into the verdurous passage she went. The path eventually sloped downward, gradually carving a corridor deeper and deeper into the earth. The ground seemed to rise to meet her as she descended. She looked up at the trees, which rose ever higher, and followed their trunks down to their roots, woven in the walls of dirt at her sides. All the while, the leaves, grass, and moss whispered above her: *Who is she? She hasn't been here before...*

A bit farther down the trail, she began to hear faint, muddled hints of conversation and laughter. It sounded like a large group of people gathered somewhere in the distance, but there was no one else in that shrouded arcade. It nearly echoed, sneaking in from different directions as if to confuse her.

After a short time, she came to the end of the path. A large wooden door with a small window was set into the dirt wall that faced her. An iron latch secured the door and great metal hinges bolted it into the earth. It looked like the entrance to a hidden monastery or a secret medieval apothecary.

She walked up to the door and stood on the tips of her toes to look through the window. There was nothing to be seen but the suggestion of a continuing path and a dim, distant light amid the shapeless darkness, like the glow of a lantern behind a thin curtain. She pressed one hand to the old, rough wood, lifted the latch, and pulled.

It was stubborn. The latch released but the door would only budge. It was teasing her. Too curious to give in, she put her weight against it. The hinges creaked and the dirt crunched as it reluctantly opened. As it groaned grudgingly toward her, a gust of cool air escaped from the gap and the murmur of a distant crowd returned. This time, it was more defined and distinctly ahead of her.

She stepped through the doorway into a short tunnel, lit with torches, that opened into a vast, cavernous space. She stood at the opening and looked out at an expanse of tables and tents. People gathered and meandered while the smell of fresh baking and an intangible hint of music filled the air.

An underground flea market.
She thought it.
"This is an underground flea market..."
She said it.

It all felt rather ordinary, though she recognized an absurdity when she saw it. She walked toward the bustling spectacle, surveying the landscape. She was definitely underground, but it wasn't dark or damp. The space was open and round with a high, cavelike ceiling. Patches of grass and moss speckled the ground.

As she grew closer to the event, she was delighted by the scene that awaited her. Tall, cast iron lamp posts lined the walkways between tables and illuminated the area. Round paper lanterns floating around the ceiling cast a warm light over everything. Dozens of vendors filled tables and booths with their wares, a fascinating smorgasbord for the senses.

Everywhere she looked, there were crafts and clothing, dishware and utensils, lovely antiques and sparkling jewelry. She walked for a while without aim or intention, simply absorbing the magnificent displays. How could such a marvelous market be hidden underground?

Several tables of wonderful trinkets and beautiful figurines caught her attention. One table in particular made her pause. It was full of stone cat statues of various sizes and colors. She picked up a small crystal figure in the shape of a napping cat. It was smooth, and rounded, and graceful. She ran her fingers over the cool, sleek curves, admiring the craftsmanship. The man sitting behind the table smiled and asked her if she liked it. She told him she liked it very much, but she was just looking.

She looked down and noticed a small step peeking out from under the hem of his tablecloth. He stood up and offered her his hand. "Please, madam, allow me…" She took the step and he helped her up onto his table. There was a small empty spot, just big enough for her to stand and not disturb his cats. "Please, look around and enjoy yourself. There are so many wonderful things here!" He released her hand and gestured outward down the row.

The vendors all smiled and waved up at her as she tiptoed across the tables of captivating bits and baubles. She lifted her arms, trying to maintain her balance while she looked around. There were perfect tiny clearings for every step she took, like the tables had been expecting her.

She continued across the tabletops until she reached the end of the row where the final vendor helped her back down to the ground. She went on with her wandering, exploring row after row.

At the far end of the market, she noticed an area without many lights before a large tent that appeared to be lit from the inside. The light was inconsistent, as if it came from a number of flickering candles. She felt the same pull that she experienced at the steps that brought her to this bizarre place.

As she drew closer, she observed three or four people standing outside. Each of them paused at the entrance and went in a few seconds later. Closer still, she could hear a jaunty waltz coming from the tent. She thought she saw silhouettes shifting inside, but when she focused, they diffused. It was the same fluttering glow she noticed from afar.

She arrived at the front of the tent. The entrance had been cordoned off by stanchions connected with lavender velvet rope. A sharply dressed woman with short, dark hair and a smoking Cabriole stood before the entryway. Stone-faced and supercilious, the woman sized her up. "You may enter if you do not know who your father is."

Incredulous (and frankly, rather offended), she stared back at this cold woman blocking her way. *What is this? How could anyone know?* She was adopted, and proudly so, but she could never escape a deep-rooted longing to know where she came from.

Seeing no way around it, she nodded. The woman's eyes softened and she smiled sympathetically, nodding in return. Placing one hand over her heart, the woman unlatched a section of velvet rope and gestured an invitation.

She walked past the smoking woman, into the mysterious tent. Suddenly, she was twirling in a flowing, sparkling gown. Someone took her hand and spun her. She whirled from one person to the next, then the next, and the next again. It was a splendid, elegant dance. An opulent chandelier and dozens of candelabras cast their swaying shadows upon the draping walls.

It was warm and soft as if they were floating in the smoke of the candlelight. Carefree and indulgent, their laughter echoed and lingered about like the music that moved their spirits. The weights that burdened their hearts were lifted away, witnessed and found guilty of their own making.

At last, she was content. Finally, her smile was real. She couldn't remember ever feeling so free. She never wanted to leave, but knew she could not stay. There are limits to these things. Eventually, reality imposes its commandments. Eventually, one wakes up.

The commotion of shimmering gold and swirling iridescence blurred, fading gently to white. The pale dawn light coaxed her from her dream and carried her into a new morning.

The First Promise of Spring

Crocus flowers bravely bloom
from beneath the soft white snow,
leaving mother's womb as warm winds blow calm,
waking sleepy flora from their deep rest.

The trees whisper quiet things through newborn air.
Buds sprout, dark red and split on top,
like tiny mouths, ready to spread wide
and sing their glorious lavender and green.

Water ripples once again, restless from months of confinement.
Depths are free now, to move as they will...
No cold, unyielding restriction
hindering the carefree motion of the waves.

New grass whistles, hushing the call of the breeze.
Flowers rise like children—small and fragile, playful and dear.
Color bleeds across the grateful land.
So long had it been barren.

Earth has given the first promise of spring.
The Mother enters the season of awakening and rebirth.
The cold of winter will slowly fade,
leaving our willing world to wake in peace.

written 02/10/06
revised 09/04/22 & 08/12/23
(and again on 1/16/24)

Yet Another Peculiar Promenade

The elevator was in no hurry during its slow, lazy descent. She felt as if she had been there forever. It didn't bother her, though. She had nowhere to be, and it was a beautiful and luxurious cabin. The walls were lined with richly carved wood about four feet high, meeting crimson velvet panels that stretched to the ceiling. Each wall had a long, shiny brass handrail with ornamental knobs on either end. The floor had cream and black tiles in a checkered diamond pattern.

She couldn't remember the last time she felt so posh. Really, she couldn't remember the last time she had even gone somewhere big enough to take an elevator. She raised her hand to the smooth velvet wall and traced the delicate damask stitching, mesmerized by the soft vibration and low hum of the engine. Finally, the elevator slowed to a stop.

Ding

The doors slid open, and she walked across the grate onto a hard dirt floor. She entered an expansive, hollow space with a high, uneven ceiling like the inside of a cave. A few hundred feet in front of her, dozens of people milled about a sizable configuration of tents and tables. Music and the aroma of freshly cooked food hung in the air.

She hadn't been going anywhere in particular but certainly didn't expect to end up in a place like this. It was familiar, yet the memory was far away. She felt like she'd been there before, but had a hard time getting her head around the idea of a flea market that happened underground.

Strolling around the pathways, she found what she expected to find in a market. It was a quaint gathering of all sorts of vendors. Some tables had trinkets, while others had crafts or old kitchenware. There were even a few antique stands and some booths with homemade pastries and clothing.

As she moved farther into the market, something odd happened. Each time she looked down at a table, then up again, something was different. Little by little, the scenery began to change. The dirt had been replaced by a tile floor. Tents slowly became store facades, and some tables turned into kiosks. Music that had been played by a small band now drifted anemically through overhead speakers. *Muzak. This must be a nightmare...*

Eventually, the space was completely enclosed. The charming, mysterious underground market was now a modern mall. It was dark and ambient, with shiny walls and intermittent flares of bronze and marble. Flat wooden benches lined the center of every aisle, adorned with vibrant ferns and monstera.

She passed a number of interesting and surprising stores: The Sock Hop, where you could buy single socks to replace the ones that get lost in the laundry; PermaPlant, where they sold plants that never need to be watered; PhastPhoodz!, which contained groceries that prepare and cook themselves; Sheds & Knavish, a bookstore specializing in stories that have yet to be written; This Is The Outfit You're Looking For, where you could walk in and everything you tried on fit perfectly and was exactly what you needed.

One particular shop, The Bee Store, caught her attention. She went inside and discovered a wonderland of wax carvings and figurines. Some were intricate and detailed, while others were smooth and elegant. Some were small and delicate, while others were tall and statuesque. Everything smelled like honey, yet she couldn't find any.

There were chunks of dried honeycomb in odd formations hanging on the walls and on the tables between figures. Some of them were dyed or painted. She wondered how wax could be formed into such magnificent art. It felt bittersweet. These fantastic pieces could so easily be smashed or melted if people didn't take care of them. All of that fine work and craftsmanship would be for nothing.

She desperately wanted to take some of those beautiful wax carvings home but realized she had no money or a safe way to transport them. She didn't even know where she was, though the thought was more intriguing than concerning.

She left the store and continued wandering that beguiling underground mall. To her alarm, someone called her name. She turned and saw a small group of colleagues approaching from a few stores away. *Where did they come from? Why were they here?* The group greeted her and shook hands, laughing and carrying on.

They explored together for a while, passing more peculiar storefronts: MoodSmoothy, where your drink changed color to match your emotions; ProtoPhoto, a photo booth that showed the way you really felt; The Smitten Kitten, a pet shop where the animals choose their humans. Everything was wonderful and unexpected.

Eventually, they went their separate ways. Her colleagues disappeared into the meandering crowd, and she made her way back to where she started. She was of two minds: One tried to analyze the strange events of the day. The other relished her adventure and looked forward to another long, relaxing ride in that lavish elevator.

The Green Man

I moved to a small town, as I often do. This one had a charm and ambiance all its own.

Though "small," in this case, was a generous characterization. It consisted of approximately five houses, all on one street. One house was caddy-corner and seemed to float off into nowhere.

It was winter, snow everywhere, yet it wasn't cold. In fact, such was its quaint, picturesque simplicity, the entire town could have been constructed inside a snow globe. Perhaps it was.

Almost immediately upon my arrival, I felt compelled to introduce myself to my new neighbors. This was notably uncharacteristic, as I could effortlessly go months without seeing or speaking to anyone. But I suppose the myth of isolation that comes with the idea of life in a small town is easily undercut by proximity.

Nevertheless, I was drawn to the house next to mine. I knocked at the door and waited. A stout, older woman answered, but before she could speak, a little girl pranced up, her long blond hair swishing from side to side.

"Hi! Who are you?" the little girl asked.

"Shush, girl," the woman snapped. "Don't talk to strangers!"

"I'm not talking to strangers!" the little girl insisted, crossing her arms. Then she looked at me quite earnestly. "Are you a stranger?"

"Well, yes," I said, "but I'm a nice one. I'm your new neighbor."

Before I knew it, I was ushered inside with a cup of tea in my hand. The little girl told me she was going to her friend's house for a birthday party but she hated her hair. She pointed to the side of her head, emphasizing a short bob cut that fell just below her ears. She said it was positively too short and she would absolutely have to wear a hair extension.

Upon hearing this, the old woman grumbled and shifted in her seat. Apparently, she did not like the idea. Still, the little girl only had one tiny hair extension, which was little more than a patch. She held the silly thing up for me to see, complaining that it stuck straight out wherever she tried to put it. She scrunched her face in disappointment.

A door opened and a man walked into the room, removing his coat. He emerged through an opening from a short hallway and placed his coat on an ornate hatstand, though I could have sworn that neither of those things were there when I arrived.

He was a tall, hardy man with a kind face and wise eyes. He wore a red and tan flannel on top of light jeans with thick wool socks—the kind you wear under boots when you shovel snow.

I knelt down toward the little girl and told her I thought her haircut was very nice, but if she wanted to stand out at her party, she should wear the hair extension "here," and I tapped on my chin. She laughed.

"I can't do that!" she said with a giggle, then skipped over to the man for a hug.

"But then you could look just like your dad," I teased. They laughed.

"Uncle," he corrected.

The man crossed the room toward me and sat on a tall stool at a large wooden table, bringing his face almost level with my own. He looked at me as though he was going to introduce himself, his body language open as if he wanted to start a conversation. Instead, there was silence. In that lingering moment, I started to take notice of him.

His beard was short, what you might have called salt-and-pepper were it not for one exception. What small patches of gray there were slowly turned to white and lavender, hinting blues and greens. It was nearly imperceptible, while at the same time plain as day. No one else seemed to notice, but I was transfixed.

Unable to avert my gaze, I watched the small patches in his beard spread and became a full gradient through all the hair on his head, but that wasn't all. My focus changed suddenly, as if looking through a magnifying glass. In the pools of color, I could see tiny flowers. Delicate leaves and petals hid among the follicles, slowly becoming more distinct as if a veil was being lifted.

I wondered what, and why, and how any of this could be happening, then felt a sudden sense of reassurance, though I don't recall if he ever spoke. Reality seemed so far away, but I managed to grasp just enough to pull my focus back and look around at the little girl who was playing contentedly across the table.

When I looked back, his hair had been completely replaced by flowers. They opened and closed, grew and receded, undulating slowly as if they were swaying underwater. In full bloom their heads were no bigger than a dime, but there were dozens of them —brilliant reds and blues, bright green leaves and vines, all shining like they were made of wax. There were even tiny butterflies flittering from flower to flower.

I must have looked as bewildered as I felt. When I met his eyes, they were deep and calm, resting above a gentle smile. He didn't speak. I watched him for a moment, mesmerized, until I managed a few words.

"You're a... you're an ecosystem!"

"Hmm," his brow furrowed slightly, contemplating me. He chuckled.

"You're a world," my voice broke. I don't know why but I began to feel emotional.

I reached out carefully to touch one of the flowers, to feel what my eyes couldn't believe. Running my fingers over and through them, so carefully, so gingerly, they felt unlike any flower I had ever touched. They were soft, smooth, thick, like they were made of silicone or soft rubber. Yet, it wasn't altogether different from running fingers through hair.

I was filled with a wonder I didn't recognize, like I was let in on some important secret—allowed to witness a power I wasn't supposed to know. However, it occurred to me that the man, as well as the flowers could probably feel and may be affected by my touch. It also occurred to me, after an uncomfortable amount of time, that I had not actually asked his permission to touch him.

Quickly pulling my hand back, I looked him in the eyes again and he spoke.

"It's alright. It doesn't hurt them. It just is. They're not as delicate as they look."

"But they're alive," I answered. "How do they not get hurt when you wear a hat or lay on them?"

He smiled and his eyes wandered, as if searching for the right words to explain. "They simply are."

"But how do you do everyday things?" I continued. "Don't they get in the way?"

"Well, I wonder…" he murmured, raising his eyebrows, a mischievous glint about him.

He kissed me.

I found myself pulled in. I felt the flowers around his mouth and chin clear away allowing our skin to touch. I found my hands in his hair once again. Still gentle, still careful, I could feel every flower. I felt them bloom. I felt them blossom. I felt their life and their freedom.

I woke up slowly, the air comfortably chilly, though my hand was still warm. It took a moment to realize I was gently rubbing my fingers together. As awareness crept in, as it stubbornly does upon waking, I could still feel a tiny flower. Just barely.

All My Endings

End all my endings, please, high summer Sun.
Lighten my days and awaken my dreams.
Begin my beginnings, I've only begun.
Or take what is left of me. Make me unseen.

Question my answers. How can it be so?
Pay some attention—I'm falling behind.
Your heights are too lofty for me here below.
The wind cannot carry me that far this time.

Hasten my healing, oh, cool winter Moon.
Shine in the darkness and diamond the night.
Illuminate softly this calm, snowy dune,
and hallow my prayer in the tide of your light.

Quiet my yearning, you warm vernal rain.
Wash away levees that burden my mind.
Your waters could sweep me away in their vein,
but I have a home yet to find.

Part II:

Games We Play

Introduction to The Dictionary Game

I never thought there could be a benefit to writer's block, the unrelenting antagonist in so many creative endeavors. That fickle curmudgeon can't be bribed with caffeine, liquor or any amount of swearing (though trying can yield its own rewards). It has, nevertheless, presented interesting opportunities that have led me to wonderful things.

I was introduced to an exercise designed to overcome writer's block by stimulating the creative flow, using random entries in a dictionary. This exercise, which quickly became a game my friends and I played for fun, involved two or more people, each receiving two arbitrary numbers: The first number represented the page to which one would open. The second number represented the word to which one would count.

Each participant made note of their word, set a time limit, then wrote something, anything, using or inspired by that word or its definitions. After the agreed-upon time, everyone shared their writing and a workshop would begin.

The beauty was that there were no restrictions on what could be written. I produced a number of poems, short stories, essays, even song lyrics while playing The Dictionary Game, as we called it. Occasionally, all I managed to squeeze out was a simple haiku. Sometimes it didn't work at all and the empty page would get the best of me. However, the fun was in the playing. At the very least, we often learned new words.

Syringe - *n* - **1**. A hollow, cylinder-shaped piece of equipment used for sucking liquid out of something or pushing liquid into something, especially one with a needle that can be put under the skin and used to inject drugs, remove small amounts of blood, etc. **2**. - *v* - To spray liquid into using a syringe.

A pack of liars
Brevity of injection
A sack of nonsense

Proceeding slowly
A constant inward pressure
Invading our trust

Insidiously
The long game of deception
Sneaks its weathering

False profundity
Who will be the first to rise?
Are we what we hate?

Self-Abandoned - *adj.* - Lacking self restraint.

There are monsters here.
Dwelling beneath and lurking,
                    lurking.

Deep waters pervade the underneath —
          rude and murky,
          hiding beasts that surface, laughing,
                              laughing.

There are dragons about.
Smoldering danger and wickedness, flying,
                              flying.

Opportunistic fires blaze hot and cold —
          billowing smoke and ash,
          obscuring the light, lying,
                              lying.

There are goblins here.
Ghastly spirits and phantoms, waiting,
                              waiting.

Ghoulish remnants, such flotsam —
          all spoiled and loathsome.
          Every shadow a memory, haunting,
                              haunting.

There were heroes here.
Stalwart strength and truth of heart, failing,
                              failing.

Beset by chaos, wrought with grief —
          weary and apathetic.
          The will to resist our darkness, fading,
                              fading.

Sanguinary - *adj* - (*Archaic*) **1.** Full of or characterized by bloodshed. **2.** Bloodthirsty.

Such empty permanence
The final answer of far too many questions

A quick crusade or a fleeting coup
A lasting legacy of dread

Empty quivers and broken arrows spent
Blades dripping contempt and cruelty

So many lights gone out
There is potential gone for good.

Program Director - *n* - A radio or television station director who selects, plans, and schedules programs.

Pressing the buttons, a perfect clickety-clack.
Very important work is being done.
Turning the dials: revolve up for more, down for less.
      Pick your poison.

What will it broadcast today?
Do not tarry, a decision must be made.
It is busy and has very important things to do.

Adjusting the sliders, a gliding jurisdiction over inputs and such.
Staring at the screen; it's important to look like you know how to
      interpret the readings.

How much do they matter?
At the end of the day, the broadcast ends.
It pours a drink and writes a poem.

Flipping the toggles, a satisfying click —
Something important must be happening.
Pulling the levers, all the bells and whistles of a brand new toy.

Master of Ceremonies - *n* - **1**. One who acts as host at a formal event, making the welcoming speech and introducing other speakers. **2**. One who conducts a program of entertainment by introducing other performers.

The Entertainer

He never met a spotlight he didn't love.
The blinding flare from above, erupting pillars of light.
That glowing channel, carving silhouette caricatures.
Effigies of rehearsals and running shows.

He hadn't met a welcome he wouldn't indulge.
Bathed in the warmth of admiration.
Wrapped in that satisfying blanket of applause.
Such a din—echoing back, familiar like his heart beat.

He had yet to meet an audience he couldn't beguile.
Practice makes perfect, after all.
Enchantment is an art. Fascination, a science.
The discipline of adoration is well worth the cost.

He would never claim a moment that wasn't his.
He would watch from the wings—near, but elsewhere.
Veiled in velour, suspended with breathless anticipation.
Proud and hopeful for new talent, blooming passion.

He could always lift a spirit that was burdened.
He never knew how precious he was. Such rarity.
One who shines a spotlight, only to step outside of it.
He would pray for applause, but rarely his own.

Brachylogy - *n* - **1**. Brevity of diction. **2**. Concise or abridged form of expression.

The dumbing down
The phony crown
The sorry clown did see

A simple sin
An eerie din
A loathsome reverie

When silence breaks
And no one takes
A grain with what they heard

We lose it all
And let it fall
The thought before the word.

The Thought Before the Word

odd, foggy nebula
abstract painting of intention

an elusive instant
the moment it manifests
when idea becomes real

thoughts become things
potential truth lies in wait
communication may begin

a tricky business

thoughts get stuck
so many on a narrow path
so many colliding, conflicting words

words are absurdly small containers for their meanings
yet we try to fit them in—to do our bidding
we open our mouths, hoping they comply
sounds to syllables to sentences

                    language

                                        comes

                                                        out

        sound always has consequences

The Consequence of Sound

skipping, hopping
nimble and resonant waves

tripping, falling
cascading and concussive vibrations

playful and benevolent
like a clement breeze that rustles through leaves

sinister and destructive
like an errant echo that causes rockfall

with a whisper of verity
kindness in the breath of a voice

with a venom of intention
poison on the tip of a word

a game of understanding
one may sound like another
an opposite or an enemy

a struggle with meaning
one thing or the other or both
the ambition of expression

a tricky business

words get stuck
bottleneck in a rush to say our part
syllables to syntax to semantics

sounds mingle and grapple for influence
consonants only pretend to get along

a cunning onomatopoeia
a divine dissonance
just listen

Path of Thorns

These sails are shorn in tatters, every storm a whip and fray
Resilience speaks its curses, every burden has its way
All weather worn and weary, setting out on narrows new
The journey sets its hurdles high
                    and on the road are you

A fortress of benevolence, eroding by degree
A cruel and rusty credo breeds a hollow enmity
But mercy is as mercy does, and kindness begs its coup
Redemption lays a taxing path
                    and on the road are you

A thousand insecurities have left their mark in turn
And every disappointment haunts a heart it didn't earn
So each betrayal spins a web and conjures ghosts on cue
And footing is a fickle thing
                    but on the road are you

She never was a girl who wasted time on silly things
He never was the boy who loved his god and found his wings
Our spirit rocks at such a clip and tosses like the sea
To each their own to hoe their row
                    and on the road are we

Boy Mercury

"Boy Mercury, shooting through every degree.
Oh, girl, dancing down those dirty and dusty trails.
Take it hip to hip, rocket through the wilderness.
Around the world, the trip begins with a kiss."
~from "Roam" by The B-52's

I am a Gemini, born on the 19th of June
Guided by the planet Mercury
I fly with Hermes

I know who I am on occasion
I know who I want to be some days
Mostly I recall who I was

I remember a life
Like watching from the outside
A visiting ghost, just looking in

There he was, a boy
This skipping, running, flying boy
Like a lightning strike through the world

Chasing fancies
Singing always, never stopping
Dancing, twirling, jumping

Silliness and innocence
Whimsy and mischievous smiles
Laughter that echoed and filled his mother's heart

Curious but careful
Sensitive but resilient
Both aware and indifferent

So much smiling, sometimes crying
Always loving
Always wanting

VHS tape obsessions and imaginary heroes
Little Mermaids and Last Unicorns
Benevolent cowboys and space princesses
Samurais and sailors

Memories of grocery store samples
Airshows and golf carts
Monarchs over bike trails
Pink shells and willow beaches

So many memories
Reflective facets and glinting fragments
Bits and baubles, all adding up

A singular and joyful spirit
A rare and extraordinary heart
He was magic
          He was Boy Mercury

On Cats

or, Fluffy is a Vicious Killer

A shake and a pounce
A wide-eyed beast, frozen in excitement
A manic burst
A frenzied fluff

A measured indifference
A supple stretch, flaunting liquid body
A languid lay
A perfect puff

An insatiable lust
A wanton hunt; pastime of the gods
A razor touch
A fearsome feature

A jump, a leap
An effortless flight, heedless of gravity
A flawless landing
A queenly creature

A purring loaf
A charming voice; mysterious language
A chirp and a trill
A coiling spring

A fickle friend
A guarded trust, quite conditional
A flirting familiar
A hungry thing

Windmills

We're tilting at windmills
What ghouls do we see?
What monsters lie waiting?
What specters roam free?

Delusions of grandeur
Extravagant airs
We tilt at these windmills
Delusive fanfares

A joust and a pageant
With lunacy's lance
We tilt at these windmills
A paranoid dance

A fine Dulcinea
A phantom of lust
We tilt at that windmill
Our diamonds and rust

We suckle tradition
The way, just because
We tilt at this windmill
What is always was

We spit at oppression
but seldom agree
We tilt at these windmills
and trust what we see

We hide behind curses
Our virtue devised
To tilt at that windmill
Our cruelty disguised

We burn all the witches
We judge them with fire
We tilt at the windmills
but never the pyre

The effort was noble
but all was for scorn
We've tilted at windmills
since the day we were born

All's well that ends well
And thus we belie
We'll tilt at those blades
'til the day that we die

We're tilting at windmills
What ghouls do we see?
What monsters lie waiting?
What specters roam free?

All's Well That Ends

All's well that ends well
and ends all that was
Well ends the story
 which ends just because

All the fair maidens
 and ev'ry young lad
Fecund and supple
 gone wilted and sad

All's well that ends well
and ends all that was
Well ends the beauty
which ends just because

All the king's horses
and all the king's men
gambled with fealty
and rode to their end

All's well that ends well
and ends all that was
Well ends the kingdom
which ends just because

All in good fortune
and each one in turn
Each seed is sewn
every deficit earned

All's well that ends well
and ends all that was
Well ends the journey
which ends just because

Lakes Into Oceans
(A Song)

These eyes are just lakes, not an ocean to speak of.
The whites are just sands on the shore.
If you were to swim and get pulled to the deep of this lake,
would you care anymore?

I'm writing a story. I'm writing a song
that I hope will not fill with regret.
And one day, this lake, it might spill to the ocean,
but I haven't finished it yet.

These words are just sounds, only symbols and pen strokes.
Their meanings are waiting, concealed.
If you were to translate and get to the root of these words,
would their worth be revealed?

I'm writing a story. I'm writing a song
that I hope will not fill with regret.
And one day, this song, it might float to the surface
but I haven't finished it yet.

This dream is so frail and its likely to vanish
like vapor or memory or hope.
If I were to ask for some vain absolution in spite,
would it be just to cope?

I'm painting a picture, I'm playing along,
and along in a tiresome vignette.
And one day, this story may fill to the borders
but I haven't finished it yet.

written 03/15/14
revised 08/13/23

Bah, Bah, Black Sheep

Bah, bah, black sheep
Have you any thoughts?
    no, sir
        no, sir
            no, sir
                naught

None for the scholar
None for the tramp
None for the whipping boy who takes it like a champ

Bah, bah, black sheep
Have you any thoughts?
    no, sir
        no, sir
            no, sir
                naught

None for the master
None for the slave
None for the working man who labors to the grave

Bah, bah, black sheep
Have you any thoughts?
    no, sir
        no, sir
            no, sir
                naught

None for the children
None for the slain
None for the bomber who is strolling down the lane

Bah, bah, black sheep
Have you any thoughts?
    no, sir
          no, sir
               no, sir
                    naught

Sleight of Hand

So what did your cruelty deliver?
And what has your kindness undone?
A sleight of the hand makes a slave for the land.
We have ended before we've begun.

To what do you owe your successes?
And what has your apathy won?
And where are we now? Just a lesson on how
they diminish us under the gun.

Apex
(Burden)

a grandeur delusion
a hubris in kind
entitled and mindless
a dueness divine

and never we mind it
or care in the least
to pass on our burden
or burden the beast

a prideful transgression
and par for the course
when not once did the rider
deserve his good horse

I'll Never Tell

Heavenly presence
    Ecclesiastic grace
      existing on a plane apart from our own
        separate, but near

Heavenly presence
    Ecclesiastic voice
      like warm wind, soft sunlight through glass

Heavenly presence
    Ecclesiastic eyes
      sapphires and stars and things alight with passion

Heavenly presence
    Ecclesiastic face
      indelible smile, a visage to haunt the memory

Heavily presence
    Ecclesiastic heart
      one so rare, a decency abiding like truth

Heavenly presence
    Ecclesiastic skin
      I will wish, I will want, I will hope
        but I'll never tell

Originally written in Winter '05
Revised 11/22 & 9/23

The Hollow

I'm absolutely certain that it's been 200 years since you died.
But calendars and commitments, grocery trips and rent checks suggest differently.
I was once able to count the times I dreamt about you on one hand. Then, two. Then...
A cruel abacus, using memories as beads—sliding back and forth.
Bent wires and tired frames assigning value to what could never be calculated.
Regardless, I wake up crying.
Either way, you're gone.

Time moves differently inside the hollow. Minutes feel like days. Days can feel like months. Or sometimes hours go by in the space of a single thought. Suddenly, you're snapped back to reality and don't quite know where you are, like you've been jolted awake from a bad dream. But it isn't a dream. And you haven't woken up.

The hollow starts out round, taking up as much space within you as it can. Inside, outside, above, below, it contains you as well. You can't get out of it, or even find yourself from the outside. The toll it takes is persistent and cruel.

It begins when you get the news. Your ears start to ring as your brain tells your heart. All the while, adrenaline does its best to protect you. It races around, searching for explanations—any reason that what you can't possibly believe couldn't possibly be true. Then, the silence settles in. The hollow grows.

As it turns out, no one is immune. Regardless of who we are, where we are or how smoothly we've been sailing, we're only a blink away from time-stop. At any given moment, we're all just a phone call from our knees.

It takes your breath, the hollow. Breathe in, the air gets pulled into the emptiness, allowing you enough to survive, but not enough to live. Breathe out and it hardly matters. It puts you in a stasis and makes you numb.

Nothing interesting could possibly happen. If it did, there would be no comfort in it. Guilt would accompany any joy. Every laugh would be a betrayal. After all, the one you lost can never laugh with you again.

The hollow is both captor and protector. In the din of grief, it's quiet. In the chaos of funerals and families and flower arrangements, it's comfortable. Everything has soft, hazy edges so you feel safe, though you never know you're lost.

You're surrounded by a dim, gray landscape. Memories become endless skies. Words unsaid become vast canyons. Regrets and guilt become the very mists that enshroud you, mercifully guarding against the reality that lurks in a viewing room. At the end of the day, bodies in caskets are all the same. But grief is bigger than bodies.

The hollow knows.

The hollow is tenacious, but benevolent. You may even find your way out, but there's no parade; there's no fanfare, no flashing lights or celebration. There's no finish line. It's so mundane, you barely notice. Life goes on and it moves to the back of your mind like deadlines or taxes. It never really goes away, just like grief never really goes away. It simply changes form.

Now the hollow is flat and wide. It gets out of your way and lingers, waiting in the wings. It slides under the bed, out of sight, or up against the wall like a painting. It's always there, but doesn't really exist until you look at it. It's invisible until you think about it, until you consider it.

One day, you'll observe the hollow. You'll glance at it from across the room and remember the duality you survived when your world shattered. It lives in you, after all—your quietest, most inscrutable friend. It's always there, should you need it again. And with what grace has given us, you will.

for Jordan

Days Few and Far

You died when you left.
The poison took you away—so far away…
You never had time to see the potential of what we could have
been.
But I saw. I knew. And I knew it every day after you left.
And your ghost would never let me forget.
That familiar spirit lingers and dances out the memories.
The bits and pieces of what time we could steal.
Your father's basement or my tiny, shitty apartment…
     No money, no privacy, no idea.
We were so young.

    Forever meant nothing when we had nothing.

You died when you fell.
I can only think I've been here before.
I didn't know where you were, but I begged God to let you pass.
I screamed your name and it felt like medicine.
I grasped and reached for you. I drank your memory so deep—
but you were never at the bottom of any of those bottles.
I never forgot you, but I forgave you—
    the man I love disappeared before you left.
Now the familiar ghost of you is a haunting.
Now, instead of wondering when you'll let me go,
    I'll wait for you to come back.
My heart is a house haunted.

    Forever meant nothing, now we have nothing.

Name Your Demons

Name your demons. Name them well.
Know the vassals. Know your hell.

Dance with specters, left to right.
Swaying, troubled, day to night.

Tempting, hanging, dulcet fruit—
Black of leaf and black of root.

Serve a sentence. Make it last.
Suffer present. Suffer past.

Say it righteous. Say it strong.
Give your freedom. Play along.

Sing the praises. Genuflect.
Wither weakly. Don't object.

March in tandem, blow by blow.
Off, we gather. Off we go.

Name your demons. Name them well.
Know the vassals. Know your hell.

The Light in the Hall

I think about the friends I've had.
Hourglass empty, pen in hand,
would it do to know I'm thinking of them now?

The story goes in highs and lows.
For all our joys and all our woes,
could happenstance explain it all somehow?

The spirit that resides in you,
for all the pain it's put you through—
is it worth it now to ask for greater sight?

I'll leave the light on in the hall.
If you should cry or you should fall,
I'll find my way to you and hold you tight.

I took advice from friends I knew,
but puddles that they led me through
were oceans in disguise, and had I known...

You could be in bed with enemies,
as long as there's no sign of these
emotions that I thought could be outgrown.

It's funny how the time goes by.
But if we ever learn to fly,
we'd get from *a* to *b* so safe and sound—
        and never know that we are losing ground.

The Day for Night

The brightness of the day does not agree
        with what my heart tells me to be real.
Yet, it drinks the Sun like wine,
        with abandon it cannot afford.
What a shame, when we cannot see the day for night.
What a waste that we cannot see the night for fear.

Fear of God drives the world.
Love of God…there is no finish to that thought that will do.
Love of God is ineffable…
        older and more powerful than religion…

Ancient
      Sacred
           Fearsome

The brightness of the day is where
        we allow things to grow,
        we allow things to thrive.
The night, where we leave them to fester and die…
        where we hand things away to unknowing—
        where we are afraid to celebrate life.

This is wrong.

Time of day and length of light are of no consequence.
Why should hope die in the dark?

The Short End of Twilight

We are faint as stars
    Twilight into dusk, we are children
We are faint as stars
    Twinkling in the sky, we are infinite
But you shine so bright,
    brilliant in the endlessness of this lovely night—
    endless in its emptiness, I am spinning
We are faint as stars

Abandoned Concepts

We write songs and poems, from time to time,
about life and love, loss and grief.
We decide, ultimately, which words will do.
What will define our ideas?
Minds racing every which way, spewing
notion after notion onto the waiting white.
A blank page is a stubborn foe,
an irksome obstacle.

Some ideas are more difficult than others.
Elaborating becomes a chore.
So tedious, so laborious, so exhausting.
Most ideas are given up. Lost.
They become abandoned concepts.
We decide what we think is no good.
First with trash, then with words.
Then, with people.

We leave with the best of intentions.
I'll go my way, you'll go yours.
Best wishes of luck. Live long and prosper.
Time-honored insincerities.
We, the well-wishers, ask a promise.
Will we remember to remember?
No one wants to revisit an abandoned concept.
Some are simply dispensable.

Written 06/02/06
Revised 08/26/23

In Love With the Wind
(A Waltz)

Leave it to me, I'm in love with the wind
We were gone before we could begin
It was never enough and the going was tough
So the tough packed it up and packed in

Leave it to me, I've been lost in the woods
And I can't see the forest for trees
A humbling yield and a blight on the field
But we can't love the frost for the freeze

Leave it to me, I give into lament
Put your ear to the shell and you'll hear
a hollow domain, such a woeful refrain
Then the sound and the hope disappear

Leave it to me, I'm just letting it be
In a tempest that shatters the land
And left in the wake is the grace that I fake
And a faith that I catch-as-catch-can

Leave it to me, I'm in love with the wind
Yet another to take on the chin
We were never enough and the going was tough
So the tough packed it up and packed in

Silhouettes

will my hopes outweigh my fears
    silhouettes and shapes made long ago
        monsters I built myself
            the architect of my own shadows

      can my future survive my past
          a smoky, pernicious potion
       this poisonous mix of history
choking potential and jeopardizing prospects

           do my gifts justify my needs
a person outside of their element
          comfort zones more delicate than they've earned
      more precious than they deserve

will my tears outlast my crimes
      for every wrong, an open wound
          every sin, a withering beacon
              guilt consumes but offers nothing

      will my burdens forgive my shortcomings
can my words carry the weight of my prayers
         the
       answers
           are
             in
                the
                  o
                u
              t
            l
          i
        n
      e
    s

Guilt Is a Wicked Ghost

Guilt is a wicked ghost.
Truth, an enchantment more sinister.
Curious instruments, both—
  though truth serves us better.

Guilt is a wanting wraith.
Faith, a hopeful deliverance.
Gluttonous bullies, both—
  collectors of skeletons.

Guilt is a wicked ghost.
Truth, an enchantment more beguiling.
Curious weapons, both—
  but truth does battle best.

Guilt is a woeful word,
a searching, mournful cry.
Hearts reach out in vain.
  It isn't ours to know why.

The Snowflake & the Avalanche

"All it takes for evil to succeed is for good men to do nothing."
~ *unknown, contested and important*

fear is a worrisome predator
accompanied by despair, his cold accomplice
they walk, hand in hand, strident and remorseless
surveying their hunting grounds
taking stock of our insecurities
memorizing our vulnerabilities

and they have their way
masquerading as wisdom, a peacock display of good nature
so we are taught to turn a cheek, then another
we are coaxed into indolence

but how could you forget a fire as it burns you?
or ignore the ocean as you drown?
the enormity of the inevitable looms
an insurmountable deluge quickens
and you are just a snowflake in an avalanche

but fear is a common bully
and what could be more common than a bully?
creeping in, an insidious fool
or blustering and loud, a simple jester
and they will rely on your indecision
they will feed on your inaction

but you are one of many
we are shown that we are few, taught that we are less
we are tricked into despair
but a masquerade is just a dance, a peacock display of power

how can you ignore the need as it begs your movement?
or forget decency as it galvanizes your kindness?
there's more than one way to be dangerous.
and what better weapon?
the enormity of our potential glistens
an insurmountable force arises
and you will be a snowflake in the avalanche

Tiny Points of Light

We are tiny points of light—wandering,
    confused as to whether we are living or dying.

We are tiny flames—trembling against the dark,
    flickering and fading, shining for our lives.

We are standing on the doorstep of our own experience,
    unsure of whether we're coming or going.

We are children, wide-eyed and searching,
    vulnerable to temptation and the allure of faith.

We are caught in an eddy of absurdity,
    frantically grasping for wisdom and balance.

We are sinking in a gloomy mire, unaware of the hands,
    support at our fingertips, when we've only to reach out.

We are much more than we allow ourselves—
    voluminous spirits, transcending our limitations.

We could rise in our multitude. We could fill the darkness.
    We are tiny points of light.

Part III:

Homes We Build

Time & Dust

We were so young when this picture was taken, Morrison and I.
So young.

An old woman raised her delicate finger to a fading portrait and caressed the glass. Up and down, she traced the dim figure of the couple standing in the photograph as if they could feel her touch. In a way, she wished they could have; that her touch today would have provided some sort of comfort to them back then.

I want to say that it seems like it was only yesterday. 'Only yesterday' was a very long time ago, now.

She removed the frame from the wall and stood with it for a moment, never breaking her gaze from the empty spot it left, a modest rectangle, just a slightly different color than the rest of the wallpaper that time had faded. Time and dust.
It made her feel safe. It made her feel something she could only describe as comfort. Then, it made her feel a dull happiness. And that made her feel lonely.

Time and dust...

Breaking her trance, the woman looked at the picture, then pressed the frame to her breast. With a sigh, she turned from the wall and walked slowly toward the parlor.
Down the hall and through a creaking doorway, she entered the room. She crossed a softly colored Persian rug and settled in a large armchair next to the front window. A half-empty cup of herbal tea from the day before still sat on the small wooden table next to her. The smell of it made her wince.

You always used to get your trousers in a bunch over that, Morri. "Would you finish a damn cup of tea?" you'd say. Sometimes I'd do it just to get your goat. You knew it, though. You were always good-natured about things.

The woman cast her attention to the picture again, resting it in her lap. She stared down at it, angling it slightly to avoid the glare from the evening Sun. Pulling the cuff of her sleeve over her hand, she brushed a bit of dust and web from the glass. It did little for the image, but it made her feel better—as if she were cleaning it up and keeping the memory tidy, as if she could remember it more clearly.

She noticed a slight halation in the corner of the photograph, just above the trees where the sun came through. It was funny, the details she had missed over time. She had never given it much thought until that moment. The picture had been taken by their neighbors at the time, on a particularly bright day in the spring when they were tilling their first garden. They had only been married for a year.

This house was a piece of trash. It was. We had never seen such a fixer-upper as this, but we bought it anyway. We were young and eager.
You said you liked a challenge. I said you liked your pocketbook free of that realtor.
But it was ours.

She could almost see the picture move, as though she were watching the memory play out before her. She could feel the breeze, the warmth of the sunlight. The smell of trimmed grass and fresh, tilled earth filled her senses as she closed her eyes. She took a slow, deep breath, letting it all in.

I miss the way my hair felt when it brushed over my shoulders while we gardened.
"My silly girl with silly hair," you'd say. You'd sweep up my wayward locks and pin them back again if my hands were dirty.
I miss that passion we had for gardening. And laughing. And living…
Things were always so difficult, but we never let it keep us from living. We were free spirits, I suppose.
I miss that freedom, Morri.

Memories of their past flooded to her, then. Memories of how happy they had been, how they laughed together. Memories of the hard times, which were plentiful, and how many times they could have left. She chuckled quietly, thinking about it.

She always wanted to go to school, but a quickly growing family put an end to that dream. She would always tell herself it was because times were different then. Her family came first, and that was her duty. She would never trade the life she made for anything—but she would always wonder.

Fifty years, Morri.
Fifty years, we've lived in this house. Well, I've lived in this house.
You've been gone for...
Where did you go, Morrison?

She looked at the photograph once more, studying her features. She had nearly forgotten the details of their faces at that age. She was almost certain she always looked as she did now. Time and age had seen to her assuredness—years and years of slow decay and waning beauty. Her eyes felt heavy then, as a wave of melancholy came over her. She was suddenly aware of the stillness of the room.

Well, Morri, now I've got the mopes.

Rising from the chair and stepping slightly to the right where an orange mirror hung, the old woman faltered briefly, then corrected herself. She looked up hesitantly from the photograph, as if her eyes did not want to meet the eyes that would be looking back at her. What a pity to be faced with reality after dwelling in such a fond memory.

Her reflection seemed just as hazy as her memories, yet it struck her. Where silky, endless red hair had been, there was now a puffy, peppered mop. Her once smooth, pale skin was now jaded and soft. Years of laughter had taken their toll around her mouth and eyes, and though she had aged well, the sight was still disheartening.

The woman stepped back to the worn, empty space on the wall. It looked as if the wall needed the photograph—that final, still moment to hang in place with all the other memories their years had gathered.

She raised the frame and carefully replaced it to its rightful spot. It seemed the wall needed it as much as she did.

With one hand still on the photograph, she gently ran her fingers over the surface of the glass. It was smooth and comforting, though only to her touch.

Were we not brave? Sometimes I wish we had been braver.
We could never uproot our lives for the sake of our children. Was that right?
Did we make the right choice?
There's only so much you can learn in one place, Morri.

The woman traced the figures once again, taking in every detail. Her eyes narrowed then, dimming with a slight glint of nostalgia. She smiled weakly and sighed, turning from the photograph on the wall. It was time to let the memory rest.

Diamonds and rust, Morri.
Time and dust…

The Lilac & the Blackberry

To be fair, I've never met a tree I didn't like.
I believe they are memory itself.
Always there, always present.
Long before, long after.
Scarcely noticed but always watching.
Silent witnesses to the life that moves around them.

The blackberry tree on the edge of the neighbor's yard
　　peeked over the fence onto our property,
　　generously sneaking its fruit for our enjoyment.
The berries would fall and for a fleeting few days,
　　half the yard would smell like jam.
It mingled with the soft presence of lilac, floating through the
　　sticky air, heavy with heat.
On the odd mild day, a merciful breeze would
　　carry the scent throughout the still, shady rooms—
　　lending just a slight allure to the lazy haze of the summer air.

Honeysuckle bushes lined the house across the street
　　and filled our tiny neighborhood with fragrance—
　　such soft, unassuming sweetness,
　　a gift from their pale, delicate flowers.
We would walk along the road on the edge of their yard,
　　gently running our fingers through the leaves and over the
　　petals.
Hands candy-coated, covered in pollen.
I would raise them to my nose and breathe deep.
It was like perfume.

It's amazing, the things you take for granted—
　　the things that pass you by when you're young and selfish,
　　unable to recognize the beauty before you until it fades.

Hating those seemingly endless summers in a small country house,

no reprieve from the thick, stifling heat.
Then time lends perspective and one can remember more kindly,
    allowing other details to recur.
Now I wish I could be there again.
The smell of grass, old wood and summer flowers.
The perfect memory of gauzy curtains,
        swaying optimistically in the warm wind
        —humidity and dust lingering in the air—
        drifting in the light in such a way...
Looking out my bedroom window,
        across the property to the lilac trees.
There was something romantic about the lilac trees.
Comforting.
I was home.

Venus in the Night

Venus, in the night, came out to play
Mercury said "We don't play that way"
but there were two of him and she did glow
so they had a party

When the Sun went down, and the Moon came 'round
all the things they saw could have burnt the ground
Scorpio stung through a verse
and they got it started

~ from "Zodiac," an unfinished poem,
circa 2015

We moved quietly and carefully down a long, narrow walkway. Small trees, leafy shrubs and ferns lined our route; a real-life Secret Garden path. Where it started, I couldn't say, but I will never forget where it led. I recall a sense that we had to be cautious—my friends and I sneaking from one place to another through leaves and wild growth, the path kept clear for twilight travelers by some magic, or at least a clever groundskeeper.

Reason tells me it was simply the path from one of their backyards into a park that was shared by the neighborhood. Everything else—heart, soul, memory—insists that it was a secret promenade, conjured for our adventure in order to avoid unwanted eyes and transport us to our destination.

We do embellish the memories we can't quite realize: indelible moments, romanticized as we need; circumstances mythologized, yet as real as the Sun; fixed points in time, though accounts may vary.

It was late summer and we had just graduated. Several friends and many acquaintances gathered for one reason or another. Graduation parties, going away parties, cookouts, bonfires—they all mixed together in the hurried, bittersweet clamor that ushered us from high school to college. Regardless of what brought us together, the party had ended. The guests took their leave, the parents went to bed, and the night was ours.

It was well after dark and there were only a few of us left, a perfect few. Aside from myself, there were three or four of my close girlfriends. My girls.

We decided to go to their private community park, which, of course, closed at sundown. It had been described to me as a quaint oasis in a large clearing in the woods next to the neighborhood. There would be a pond, though it was more like a small lake. Also, despite being more or less in the woods, a few houses were still in view of the park so we knew we had to be careful.

The night was still as a painting. The air was warm and mild, but the humidity mixed with it in such a way that we could actually smell the green. It rose from the leaves and lingered, thick, around us. Dirt and mulch lent an obtuse, nutty aroma to the concoction. Earth certainly spun the hits that night.

Stillness quelled every movement and every vibration, the errant sounds of rustling leaves or footsteps. Yet the air bombilated, buzzing a strange aria into the enchanted dark.

Without wind, without movement, the leaves still seemed to stir. They whispered above as we whispered below. The path was alive. It gladly received us, yet warned us not to stay.

We reached the end of the trail, pushed the branches aside, and entered the park. The ground immediately turned to sand and patchy grass, playground equipment all around us. Abandoned in the dark, it felt like we shouldn't be there, though our welcome was clear.

One of us, though I couldn't say who, caught the attention of the others and gestured toward the water. We all understood. Our tacit understanding set the events in motion—a naughty thrill, a defiant splash. Yet our youthful, self-shameful reservations betrayed our modest upbringing…our reluctance to recognize our own beauty. But this was our night, and we were in good company.

We walked toward the water, clumsily removing our shoes. There we were, right on the brink. The crest of our adventure had come. We shared a glance, took a breath, and went forth.

I turned slightly and averted my eyes to let them get into the water first. There was not a judgment between us, the familial intimacy we felt was strong. Still, the coveted status I enjoyed as one-of-the-girls was, in fact, honorary.

I wanted to see them, my glorious, powerful friends. My perfect, beautiful sisters. But it wasn't about me. It wasn't about them. It was about comfort and safety, celebrating our glory in nature with nothing to confine us.

We swam on that still, warm night. Witnessed only by the moon, its light glinting on midnight water, we shed our clothes and let them drop to the sand. We shed our worries and let them drift with the tide. We shed our skin and felt our freedom in the cool, dark pond.

The Suitcase & the Vacuum Cleaner

I've stood with a suitcase in my hand for as long as I can
remember.
I've been desperate to run.
>   elsewhere
>   anywhere
>   poof
>   like smoke

>   Desperate, but never ready.

The weight of this suitcase is bothersome.
How does one little life collect so much shit?
Such baggage.
So much resistance.
My shoulders ache and my arms are tired.

Buckles and clasps, straps and compartments.
Just imagine what you would have to pack
if you left and planned on never coming back.
The effort would be enough to make you stay, even out of spite.

I've never been able to put my finger on exactly what anchors me
where I am.
Picture frames illuminate timely passions, but they'll go on any wall.
A sofa remembers naps and company, but will sit on any floor.
A table bears the weight of endless food and conversation but is
necessary in any home.
Rugs recall feet and dancing and vacuum cleaners. Yet they'll lay,
    thanklessly trodden, wherever you go.

The burden of these bonds is interminable.
The things around me make so many rules.
Why is my shit so heavy?

Looking around, I couldn't help but ask myself, "what if?"
What if I left the places I love?
What if I left the shapes and surfaces and windows that kept me?
What if the doorknobs and bookshelves and boxsprings wouldn't
let me go?

What if I took them with me?
Would I be free?
Or would I just be elsewhere?

anywhere

poof

like smoke

Hospitality - *n* - **1**. Cordial and generous reception of or disposition of guests. **2**. An instance of such treatment.

Apartment

I'm happy here.
I am autonomous.
I am safe in my compartment.
I am anonymous.
I am unobserved.
>*Unwitnessed.*

I build walls to protect my privacy—a precious commodity.
Walls meant to withhold the world—a stalwart concealment.
I close doors to fend unfriendly faces.
Doors fortified to keep the ghosts at bay. Or keep them in…
>Locks, keys, and chains laugh at the
>handles and hinges, already embarrassed by neglect.
>They're rarely permitted to fulfill their purpose.
>They only have one purpose, the poor things.

I retreat into my fortress.
Desperate for these ramparts.
This prison of my making.
How often can I mistake complacency for comfort?
Sinking in my ship of safety…
>*Unwitnessed.*

Pretend prisons still have guards.
My protectors became my jailers.
When did that happen?
They provide the weapons that wound me, and I love them—
>Solitude, my oldest companion.
>Oblivion, my most voracious lover.
>Loneliness, my quietest friend.
>>*…my quietest friend.*

It's funny, the prisons we allow ourselves.

Until a new town.
Perhaps, a new life.
And then, a new compartment.
Perhaps, a new chance.

I look at throw rugs and bookshelves.
Coasters and painted mirrors,
Lamp posts and linen closets.
And what sort of prison is this?

A new place to hide my heart.
A new space to fill and fret.
A new hook to hang my hat.
But a house is not a home.

Lord, Give Me Green Lights

Lord, give me green lights when I leave to where I'm going
This stubborn road has long since shed its charm
Grant me full sails and smooth trails to ramble

Mama, give me grace to navigate my troubles
sight to see through darkness and transcend obscurity
courage to carry on and tend what flock I find

Papa, give me gravity to stay my line along
strength to weather my way and shake hands with my adversities
wisdom to hoe my row and accept what it may yield

Lord, give me green lights while I get to where I'm going
This course of obstacles has long since worn its welcome
Grant me wings or wheels or zephyrs swift
    and I will be king of the road

He Will Build With His Hands

He will build with his hands.
He will callous his skin.
He will look with wonder on the breathless beauty around him
and honor the death of the trees with what he makes.

He will see beauty in the ordinary.
He will find comfort in simplicity.
He will relish the imperfect surface of the unfathomable
    complexity of nature's work,
a perfect mystery he hopes never to solve.

He will learn birdsongs.
He will sing them to the plants he tends.
He will teach them to his regrets and send them on wing
to wherever regrets go when they are set free.

He will feel the wind.
He will let it take his body and lift his head toward the Sun.
He will gasp at the vastness of the sky.
He will surrender to its consuming enormity

He will make life in solitude, but never alone.
He will stand in the rain and thank God for the smell of wet earth.
He will weep in gratitude.
He will rejoice at his freedom.
He will build with his hands.

118 Palmer Ave

Sometimes we find places we belong, but cannot stay.

There's a funny, uncomfortable space between accepting the new and leaving the old. We tend the past while looking toward the future, all in a lather to manage the present. Every transition creates displacement, if only for an instant, and every displacement carries the potential for heartache.

I suppose it depends on the stakes of the situation: What was gained by leaving? What does this new destination offer? What gets left behind? Would it matter if you had stayed? Did it matter that you left? One could set these emotions aside, though I have rarely been known to be such a person.

It was a hot summer—mid-July and 90 degrees in the shade. I stood in the second story of a duplex. It was an old house, built in the mid 1800s and converted into apartments in the 1980s. There was no air conditioning, in fact there was no central ventilation at all. And if I had never believed it before, it was painfully clear at this time that hot air does, indeed, rise.

The best features of that old house were the floor-to-ceiling windows, and that day, they were all wide open, letting through whatever breeze they could catch. Though in a town known for its flat, windy landscape, I can't remember a day that was more infuriatingly still.

That was the last day, the last scrub and spruce before I turned in my keys. The apartment was empty. Everything had been moved out, aside from a mess of cleaning supplies, a box fan, a folding chair and of course, supplies for one last drink.

As miserable as it was, there was something fulfilling, even satisfying, about sweating and toiling in that sweltering heat. I was suffering for that final work, and I knew the satisfaction of finishing and the glory of an eventual shower would be worth it. I would wash it all off: the work, the sweat, the past.

To be clear, I never wanted to leave that town. I had lived there for 15 years, and I had spent more than a decade in that tiny, crummy apartment that no one knew was there.

The only entrance was behind the house, tucked into the downstairs tenant's adorable little garden, making it the perfect hiding place. That also made it a perfect prison—an unfortunate edge to that sword. Feeling both things at once and knowing their absolute truth was strange.

Still, I couldn't help but reflect on the comfort it brought me, my fortress of solitude. Every heartbreak, every happiness, every loneliness, all lingering in the air like perfume. Every memory reinforcing those rickety old walls. For all its charm and character, it wasn't a great house—but it was home.

After hours of dusting, scrubbing and sweeping, the end was finally near. Only one task remained, and that meant two things: First, it was time to spackle. Second, it was time for that drink.

I went to the kitchen where I had left the spackling kit on the counter next to a solitary plastic cup. I retrieved vodka and grapefruit juice from the otherwise empty refrigerator and poured my final libation. I raised my cup and tipped it forward, a silent toast to my old home.

With my drink in one hand and a putty knife in the other, I got to it. I started in the middle room, my little study, and worked my way out from there. I moved to the bathroom, then to the bedroom, smoothing over the dents and holes in my walls. Eventually, I ended up in the living room, the final frontier.

I began to work on the first wall and found myself thinking about that empty room. I thought about the different shapes it had taken: the sofa on one wall or another, the recliner here or there, shelves of books and movies and comforts unnumbered. I thought about how safe I felt there.

Then, I thought about all of those empty rooms. Those old, familiar rooms were an inextricable part of me. That house was an extension of my life, a character in my story. But everything was barren. It was over. I was leaving and it felt like I was standing in the hollowed out corpse of my best friend.

My fingers began to tingle and a pressure grew in my chest. I was breathing steadily, though it felt as if I couldn't catch my breath. Adrenaline surged in my guts and prickled up the back of my neck, finding its way through my sinuses and into my eyes.

The scene was absurd, like something from a movie. To say that I cried would be inaccurate. What started as a trickle of tears, slightly blurring my eyes, became a deluge. The weight of leaving hit me all at once and I was hysterical.

I would laugh about it one day. I knew that while it was happening, but I couldn't stop. I was devastated, and nervous, and happy, and hopeful and so many other things I couldn't identify—yet they were all coming out of my eyes…and out of my nose.

The proverbial floodgates had opened with a vengeance, and it was ugly. All the while, I continued spackling my walls. I had work to do, after all, and it was getting late.

I don't remember much after that. I do recall spending a moment in each room, running my hands along the walls, asking the house to be good to its next family. I don't remember leaving, but I remember dropping my keys in the landlord's mailbox on my way out of town. I don't remember that shower I was waiting for, but I remember waking up the next day feeling like I had been run over by my U-Haul. At the same time, it felt like I had put punctuation at the end of a very long sentence.

I left a piece of myself in that town, an indelible revenant. I also left the rest of that vodka in the refrigerator as an offering to whatever came next. I hope the renovators were able to put it to good use.

Triptych

Three ballerinas dancing in a row
Two in pink and one in gold
Hither came in paint and frame
An art without an age

My grandma's house was full of old, beautiful things, much like my memories of spending time there. I remember her piano, luxurious paintings, a marble-top buffet and pretty china cabinets. All around were glass trinkets and antique ceramic figures.

The most abiding memory is of three small paintings that hung on the wall above her bed—each one, a different ballerina in an elegant pose. They were pastels, soft and dreamlike, but they were hazy and surreal, like dusty chalk drawings.

When I was little, we would sit in her bed before we went to sleep, looking at Winnie the Pooh picture books and singing the Tigger song, or she would sing Beauty and the Beast until my eyes were heavy. All the while, I looked up at those paintings. They made me feel calm, yet a little sad. While they were beautiful and serene, there was something wistful about them, something just out of reach. They were so poised, but vulnerable.

They filled me with wonder. Thinking back, when I looked at them, I could smell dried roses and face powder...and a whiff of perfume.

My grandma left her house to my uncle, so after she died, I lost track of those paintings. They would pop into my head every now and then, but I always forgot to find out what became of them. 25 years later, my uncle passed away and we were forced to sell the property. My mother asked if there was anything I wanted from the house before we sold everything, and I finally remembered.

For 25 years, those lovely pastels had been in my mother's hallway closet. They had been packed away in a box of items she couldn't decide what to do with, but couldn't bring herself to throw away. It turns out they were never as far away as I imagined.

A sprightly twirl, a springing leap
Silken slip and tulle in pleat
Beauty graced and bodice laced
A bird within a cage

The paintings originally belonged to my great-grandmother. They were among many similar decorations, a detail that would not go unappreciated. Great-Grandma Aubry was a kind and quiet woman, and in spite of her aprons and neatly pressed house dresses, a carefree spirit was near, beneath the surface.

My mother always wondered if her grandma fantasized about being a dancer. She would imagine her waiting until nobody was home, then flitting about on pointed toes and waving her hips as she cleaned and carried on with her housework.

She did love to dance—in fact, they used to call her "Legs Aubry." Every once in a while, she and her husband would have friends or neighbors over for dinner and cards. She didn't drink much, but Great-Grandma Aubry loved a good beer and when she got to sipping, and the music was just right, she would swish her skirt and kick up her legs. They would all laugh, but she felt a freedom that nobody else noticed.

Applause, applause, a fleeting show
A flit, a float on pointed toe
But all is dust and you are just
a figure on a stage

I've always wondered who they were, those dreamy effigies. What were their names? Where did they come from and what were their lives like? Did they know each other? All in a row, they danced, separated only by wall and frame.

Where were they? What ballet were they performing? I could never hear music when I looked at them, but I knew it should be there. My mind made space for an orchestra, then let well enough alone.

I wonder if they were real dancers. Maybe they were models. Maybe they were nobody at all, simply creations of their artist's imagination.

I've thought about them often over the years. It was strange to finally see them again. They looked different than they did in my hazy childhood memories—each of them more realized and expressive than the blurry figures I remember. There they were, my enchanting dancers. They fit right back into my memories like the last piece of a puzzle I had forgotten to finish.

Now they live with me. Whenever I pass them on my wall, I still think about who they might have been. I wonder what happened to them.

Perhaps they're still waiting in the wings?

Three ballerinas dancing in a row
Two in pink and one in gold
Hither came in paint and frame
A story on a page

A Ragtime in the Old West End

After I left Bowling Green, I stayed with a friend for a few months while I searched for a new apartment. He lived in Toledo's Old West End, an historic area with neighborhoods full of brick roads, beautiful Victorian and Edwardian homes, and tall brownstone townhouses. I was lucky enough to reside in one of them—a three level masterpiece of hardwood floors, high ceilings, elegant staircases and stained glass.

To say the least, my first week was an adjustment. Something I've heard, but never fully experienced, is that old houses are full of noises. This one had them in buckets: creaks and groans, the odd drip or rattle. Already feeling unnerved in a new place, the sounds didn't exactly put me at ease, though I eventually got used to them. They faded into the background and became part of the house's charm.

One of our neighbors was a warm, eccentric woman in her late fifties. She had long, wild auburn hair and always wore kaftans or spangled knit shawls, swishing about in her garden or reading on her front porch. You got the feeling that she made the best cookies and if you ever went over to talk to her, you weren't leaving without one.

After a few days, sounds from next door began to creep in. Every once in a while, her nieces and nephews visited while their parents traveled for work. I would hear the children laughing and running up and down the stairs, the muffled pitter patter of socks on wood. People complain about hearing their neighbors, and I suppose that's fair, but this made me smile.

It reminded me of the sounds of childhood and a happy home. I grew up in a small community near a park and a daycare. The sound of children playing was ubiquitous, so much that I associate it with warmth and security. It's easy to forget how fortunate we are, and sometimes it's important to allow ourselves a reminder.

Every week or so, the faint, dull sound of a piano found its way through the walls. It was always pretty but a little clunky, and occasionally the player would stop in the middle of songs. Experience informed me of exactly what I was hearing: piano lessons. Listening to those musical apparitions brought back wonderful and complicated memories. It was amusing, though rather humbling, to hear them from the outside.

Less frequently during my stay, the piano would start, but more full-bodied and masterfully played. It typically began with a jaunty ragtime, then a slow rag, and continued on to beautiful classical pieces. It was hypnotic. I couldn't help but stop and listen, forgetting about whatever I had been doing. I would rest my head back against my chair and stare out the window into the community gardens, thinking about how much I missed the feeling of ivory keys beneath my fingers.

The day before I moved out, I went next door to say goodbye to our neighbor and thank her for being so welcoming. When I told her how much I enjoyed listening to her play the piano, she looked puzzled. She held out her hands and told me what arthritis had done to her fingers. She hadn't played the piano or given lessons in many years. In fact, as far as she knew, her piano hadn't been tuned or played by anybody in over a decade.

I didn't know her very well, and I was woefully short on time, so I did my best to suppress the chill that ran through my body. We looked at each other for a moment, neither of us knowing how to continue. I apologized and suggested that it must have been coming from my neighbors on the other side. Nonetheless, "Thank you," and "Take care," and "I'll miss coming home to your beautiful garden," and "You're so sweet, honey. Be well!"

I went back inside the townhouse and continued packing. I didn't know what to think, but I felt as though I was missing something. I know what I heard and I know where it came from. It only happened when I was in rooms that shared her walls. It was a mystery I knew may never present an answer, but I took one last shot.

Later that evening, I poured two substantial glasses of wine and waited in the kitchen for my roommate. When he came home, I descended on him like an investigating detective. I told him about my experiences and my conversation with our neighbor. He stared at me for a moment, incredulous, then took a deep swig of red.

Kevin had lived in that townhouse for just over twenty years. A musician himself, he bonded quickly with his new neighbor. Not long after he moved in, she invited him to a party celebrating a visit from her best friend, a distinguished pianist from San Francisco. They enjoyed a luxurious dinner, a bar to tempt Dionysus himself, and a night of laughter and dancing, all under the spell of his extraordinary skill at the piano bench. His passion was jazz, which he played with glee, but he teased and tugged the heartstrings of his listeners with whatever he played.

Soon after, her friend was diagnosed with a merciless and incurable illness. Knowing that he was dying, he visited her every few months of the following year until he was too sick to travel. He would sit at her piano and tickle out a bouncing ragtime or bolster a dramatic dirge.

My heart broke, but rather than splintering into pieces, it wrapped around those memories. I wanted to be sad, but I couldn't. Instead, I felt wonder and reverence. His spirit visited the last place his body felt whole and carefree—the last place he could cling to life and at the same time let it go. He plays his music into eternity.

I was allowed to hear it.

Queen of the Cemetery

I hadn't been home in months.
Home. I couldn't call it that anymore. Still, there I was.

I moved out of that town in July and took my life elsewhere.
At that point, it was almost November—I could have reached out
and touched it. Admittedly, it hadn't been that long.

Practicality will tell you that only three months had
passed. What practicality fails to reckon is that there's no such thing
as "only" when you miss something every day.

It was, in fact, 104 days that filled up and flew by. It was also
104 times I couldn't make myself go back, though it would have
been easy. It was 104 tiny withholdings leaving 104 tiny wounds.

On this day, however, Day 105, I had an appointment. Tying
up loose ends, I suppose. Necessity finally outweighed my
resistance, and there I was.

Obligations aside, I had most of the day free and I was home.
Home. I went for coffee at my favorite café, strolled around
downtown for a bit, then headed toward the main attraction, my
favorite place in the city.

I entered through the stately iron gates of the Oak Grove
Cemetery, nestled safely somewhere the Bowling Green State
University campus. It was always my sanctuary. I would take long
walks, watch the sunlight dance between the trees and just be quiet
with the gravestones, and there we were again.

It was a perfect autumn day—the kind that you would imagine
to be best for taking a thoughtful walk around a graveyard. It was
peaceful and calm. The sun was shining, the trees had started
turning, the air was just starting to chill and the wind was earthy
and sweet like leaves.

I had been once or twice around the grounds and I could feel
my knees start to ache. It was a small cemetery, but the layout of
the paths made it quite a walk if you explored them all. Everything
rose slightly from the edges of the property toward a hill in the

center. At its crest awaited a grand circle of trees, a tidy ring of clean stone benches, and a tall marble monument. It was beautiful, but my knees still ached (thank you, 36). In any case, I've never had much time for monuments or perfect circles.

The Walk had been quiet so far. One or two people had been in and out, but for the most part I was alone—as much as anyone can be alone in a graveyard. It was exactly what I wanted. It was exactly what I needed. The stillness and the magic of that place embraced me again. My old friend.

Looking around, I couldn't help but wonder what it would have been like if I had stayed. What could my life have been if I had done things differently? What if I had never met her? What if I hadn't dated him? What if I hadn't wandered into that new bar and found my people? What if I hadn't met my people in a bar? It was all horribly maudlin.

I never truly thought I would leave, so I never thought I would have to add it all up. Math is always sensible, but it never actually explains anything. One grave should equal one person, one soul. But it really equals one, plus x, where x is the amount of people who visit a gravestone or simply walk in a cemetery to be at peace among them.

I can still call a town "home." I can still miss it. But in reality, I was there alone. It became home out of habit. The people that had made Bowling Green a home for so long were long gone. They married, moved, died—whatever it may have been. I've tried to deconstruct it, to make it make sense for as long as I can remember— but I've never been good at long division.

About a mile away, the university marching band started their practice. The sound crept in, echoing over the hills and through the cemetery gates, bouncing between the headstones. I could almost see them shift uncomfortably, like sleeping cats that stir and shoot reproachful looks when disturbed.

Oh, the sounds of a small college town in the autumn. It was pretty dense, the band playing chord after chord. The heavy-handed but well-meaning brass section took the melody. There was something antagonizing about it. I knew what it was, but I didn't know why. I recognized the tune but the words wouldn't come. It was a little anachronistic—pop songs in a cemetery.

I wandered a little longer, letting everything wash over me. I imagined the ghosts and spirits laughing at the irony of it all. They would roll their eyes at someone walking by—so introspective, so reverent, so affected. They would chase and huddle around a rule breaking visitor who was smoking on the grounds, attempting to waft a secondhand fix from the cigarette.

As if from nowhere, it hit me. It was Dancing Queen. The band was playing Dancing Queen, by ABBA. There I was, philosophical and pensive. Then, suddenly, Dancing Queen. It was quite a moment: my pace giving into the beat, my head bopping a bit, my hands involuntarily miming the piano parts.

I imagined the ghosts of the BGSU cemetery, desperate for a dance, following me in their burial best to get down to that clumsy disco. I can only hope that the dead have a better sense of humor than we do—because it made me smile. And there we were.

Animal Crackers

frosted animal cookies
      pink and white
           tiny round sprinkles
                in the pantry

maeterlinck avenue
      grandma & grandpa's house
           in my fives and sixes

red toy tractor
      in the backyard
           pedals like a tricycle

wind up toy
      it danced the day into night
           a tinkling lullaby

claymation dinosaurs
      ice queen fairy tales
           and casper the friendly ghost

spaghettios for supper
      grandpa cooked
           glass of milk for strong bones

frosted animal cookies
      pink and white
           tiny round sprinkles
                in the pantry

A Silly Foal with a Silly Tail

frisking, skipping
trotting, tripping
prancing about
      "Mama, look!"
bouncing and bounding
circles around its adult
hooves dusting the air
      "Mama, look!"
springy and sprightly
scampering an innocent scamper
a silly foal with a silly tail
      "I'm with mama!" it seemed to say
in playful flicks and swishes
noticing us as we walked past the stable yard
pausing a restless pause
then cantering back to its adult
      "This is my mama!"
proud and playful
swishing, flicking
trotting, trotting
      "Mama, look!"

Ever Close to Me
(A Lullaby)

Lay down. Rest your eyes.
Rest your head, your weary head to sleep.
Close your eyes and hear the angels sing just for you.
The beauty of their lullaby you reap.

As we approach the beautiful morning,
here you lie next to me.
So far away from the break of the evening,
in my arms and ever close to me.

Sleep now. Rest your mind.
Dreaming now, but never far away.
Close your eyes and hear the angels sing just for you.
Safe and sound, and heavy are your eyes.

As we approach the beautiful morning,
there you lie, fast asleep.
So far away from the break of the evening,
in my arms and ever close to me.

As we approach the beautiful morning,
here you lie next to me.
So far away from the break of the evening,
by my side and ever close to me.

In my arms and ever close to me.

She was not talented.
She was not a mistake of nature and nurture.
She was born to it. She was meant for it.
Her voice transcended possibility. It was truth.
Her words surpassed eventuality. They were prophecy.
She was not talented.
She was Story.

What A Blessed Sky

He felt the shame upon his back,
and failure in his skin.
The love that he found, it was dead on arrival.
It emptied him out from within.
And though his heart was breaking,
he held his head so high.
He drank the Sun. He felt the wind.
He said, "What a blessed sky…"

Her body broke against the waves.
The darkness took her bones.
Her heart ripped apart on a turbulent sea
and it sank to the bottom like stones.
That sickness took her life from her,
though she refused to die.
She looked to Heaven. She prayed to God.
She said, "What a blessed sky…"

Redeem the voice that fears to speak,
although we've been through hell.
For love is hard, that much is plain
to those who do it well.
We pace our path so carefully,
but life will not comply.
We raise our hands, we bless the day,
and what a blessed sky.

Our blood, it flows the same, my friend.
It seems that we forgot.
We look for hope, we do the best
we can with what we've got.
We need to feel the sunlight—
but do we even try?
We hear the thunder, face the rain.
But what a blessed sky.

The morning glows against the hills
and wakes the world below.
The afternoon, when time stands still
and nature gets to grow—
that day was so damn beautiful
to cause these eyes to cry.
I turned away and looked above.
Oh, what a blessed sky.

In the End, Let There Be Song

Spirits long to surface
Dancing into light
Open windows calling
Distant peace in sight
Sing you now for freedom
Sing you now for home
Raise your voice unyielding
And in the end, may you belong

Cling to rugged crosses
Horns of hope abound
Circles lay unbroken
Drums and bells resound
Sing we now together
Sing we not alone
Raise our voices sacred
And in the end, let there be song

Thank You's

Thank you to my family and friends, past and present, for inspiring me and helping shape who I am.

Thank you to the wonderful folks at The Henlo Press for supporting me, believing in my voice, and putting up with me.

Thank you to Dan, Sarah, Beth & Nate, the wonderful painters and photographers who provided, and even created, art for use in promotional materials for this book.

Special thanks to Kristen & Jessi for hours of reading, listening, editing, workshopping, laughing and long walks.
This book wouldn't have been possible without you.

Finally, enormous gratitude to all the supporters and backers of this project, and to you, the reader...
This wouldn't be possible without any of you either.

Quotation & Dictionary Citations

B-52's. "Roam." _Cosmic Thing_, Reprise, 1989.

Poe (Danielewski, Annie). "Haunted." _Haunted_, Atlantic, 2000.

Saliers, Emily (Indigo Girls). "Feed and Water the Horses." _Beauty Queen Sister_, Vanguard, 2011.

"Brachylogy." The American Heritage College Dictionary, edited by Joseph Picket, Fourth edition, Houghton Mifflin, 2002, p. 173.

"Hospitality." The American Heritage College Dictionary, edited by Joseph Picket, Fourth edition, Houghton Mifflin, 2002, p. 670.

"Master of Ceremonies." The American Heritage College Dictionary, edited by Joseph Picket, Fourth edition, Houghton Mifflin, 2002, p. 852.

"Program Director." The American Heritage College Dictionary, edited by Joseph Picket, Fourth edition, Houghton Mifflin, 2002, p. 1113.

"Sanguinary." The American Heritage College Dictionary, edited by Joseph Picket, Fourth edition, Houghton Mifflin, 2002, p. 1230.

"Self-Abandoned." The American Heritage College Dictionary, edited by Joseph Picket, Fourth edition, Houghton Mifflin, 2002, p. 1257.

"Syringe." The American Heritage College Dictionary, edited by Joseph Picket, Fourth edition, Houghton Mifflin, 2002, p. 1400.

ABOUT THE AUTHOR

Mike is a native of Northwest Ohio, and has been included in several local literary journals. His first full length work, "The Dictionary Game: Stare Down the Moon," was published in late 2020.

He is also a musician with a focus on piano, voice and music production.

After attending Bowling Green State University where he majored in Sociology and vocal jazz performance, he moved to Toledo, Ohio, where he currently lives.

READ INDIE. STAY AWESOME.
MORE BOOKS FROM THE HENLO PRESS

Glass Mountain by Laura Treacy Bentley

The Dictionary Game by Mike Hornyak

Orphan Poetry by Alexis Cremeans

Extreme Human Overload by Diana Johnson

The Mother of Monsters by M.A. Elliott

A Ghost of Spring by A.B. Hooser

The Wonderfully Wild Adventures of Kana and Charlie: Monstrous Mo and the Stolen Apples by Josh Taylor, Illustrated by Jeremiah Morgan

304 Monsters by Stephen Bias

West By God by Tyler Bell

Deadly Choices: Will You Survive? | Camp Meltaway by Tiffany and Caitlyn Pace

Old Bones: Volume One by Various

A Shade of Winter by A.B. Hooser

Nora the Narwhal and her Curly Horn by Alan Maynard, Illustrated by Soma Cather

Mumblings: West Virginia Horror Stories by Caitlyn Pace

Afterwords by Stephen Bias